Over a Century of Moving to the Drum

Over a Century of Moving to the Drum

Salish Indian Celebrations on the Flathead Indian Reservation

by Johnny Arlee

Interviews with Pete Beaverhead, Blind Mose Chouteh, Mary Finley, John Peter Paul, Dolly Linsebigler, Oshanee Kenmille, Louise Combs, Bryan Brazill, and Louie Plant

Photographic essay by Rex C. Haight

Drawings by Tony Sandoval and Corky Clairmont

Edited by Robert Bigart

Co-Published by
Salish Kootenai College Press, Pablo, Montana
Montana Historical Society Press, Helena, Montana

Copyright 1998 by
Confederated Salish and Kootenai Tribes
Salish Culture Committee
St. Ignatius, Montana

Published in cooperation with the
Montana Historical Society Press, Helena, Montana

Printed in the United States of America

Library of Congress Cataloging-in-Publication Data:
Arlee, Johnny.
    Over a century of moving to the drum : Salish Indian celebrations on the Flathead Indian Reservation / by Johnny Arlee ; interviews with Pete Beaverhead ... [et. al.] ; photographic essay by Rex C. Haight ; drawings by Tony Sandoval and Corky Clairmont ; edited by Robert Bigart.
        p.   cm.
    ISBN 0-917298-57-8
    1. Salish Indians—Social life and customs. 2. Powwows—Montana—Flathead Indian Reservation. I. Bigart, Robert. II. Title.
    E99.S21A75 1998   978.6′83—dc21   98-3540 CIP

Front Cover Art: Photograph of Louie Plant by Chris Roberts, Missoula, MT; drum group drawing by Tony Sandoval, Cuba, NM; photograph of powwow camp scene by Rex C. Haight, Missoula, MT.

Back Cover Art: Photograph of John Peter Paul by Chris Roberts, Missoula, MT; photograph of Oshanee Kenmille by George Price, Ravalli, MT; drawing of Owl Dancers by Corky Clairmont, Ronan, MT.

Salish Kootenai College Press publishes books and pamphlets relating to the history and culture of the Salish and Kootenai tribes and Flathead Reservation affairs. Manuscripts have been chosen because they include valuable information that should be more widely available. The views expressed are those of the authors.

SKC Press

Publications available about the Flathead Indian Reservation

Johnny Arlee, **Over a Century of Moving to the Drum: Salish Indian Celebrations on the Flathead Indian Reservation.** Describes the early powwows or celebrations especially the Arlee Fourth of July Celebration. Includes a number of interviews with Salish elders and young people about the celebration and how it has changed.
paperback, 104 pages, 11 x 8.5, $14.95

Kootenai Culture Committee, **Ktunaxa Legends.** Traditional Coyote and animal stories of the Flathead Reservation Ktunaxa, or Kootenai Indians. Translated by the Kootenai Culture Committee and illustrated by Kootenai artists.
paperback, 400 pages, 8.5 x 11, $21.00

In the Name of the Salish & Kootenai Nation: The 1855 Hell Gate Treaty and the Origins of the Flathead Indian Reservation, edited by Robert Bigart and Clarence Woodcock. Source material and documents relating to the 1855 Hell Gate Treaty Council. Includes the text of the treaty, the full transcript of the proceedings of the council, portraits and biographical sketches of many of the Indian leaders involved.
paperback, 176 pages, 8.5 x 11, $11.00

Agnes Vanderburg, **Coming Back Slow: The Importance of Preserving Salish Indian Culture and Language.** The views of a leading Salish elder about the need to preserve Salish traditions and language.
paperback, 16 pages, 8.5 x 11, $4.00

Burton M. Smith, **The Politics of Allotment on the Flathead Indian Reservation.** A study of the political intrigue behind the 1904 legislation that forced the Salish and Kootenai tribes to sell much of the Flathead Reservation land to white homesteaders at bargain rates.
paperback, 32 pages, 8.5 x 11, $5.00

Thomas E. Connolly, S.J., **Quay-Lem U En-Chow-Men: A Collection of Hymns and Prayers in the Flathead-Kalispel-Spokane Indian Language.** Salish language Catholic hymns and prayers used on the Flathead Indian Reservation and neighboring reservations.
paperback, 76 pages, 8.5 x 11, $5.00

Robert Bigart and Clarence Woodcock, "Peter Tofft: Painter in the Wilderness." Article in Autumn 1975 issue of *Montana: The Magazine of Western History.* The story of an artist who traveled Western Montana in the 1860s and painted pictures of important historical sites such as St. Ignatius Mission, Fort Connah, Fort Owen, and Flathead Agency. Includes reproductions of the paintings of these sites.
paperback, periodical issue, 8.5 x 10, $3.00

Robert Bigart and Clarence Woodcock, "The Trans-Mississippi Exposition and the Flathead Delegation." Article in Autumn 1979 issue of *Montana: The Magazine of Western History.* Story and pictures of the Flathead Reservation delegation to the 1898 exposition in Omaha. Includes pictures and biographical sketches of Antoine Moise, Charley and Adelaide Kicking Horse, Paul and Agnes Antoine, and others.
paperback, periodical issue, 8.5 x 10, $3.00

John C. Ewers, "Iroquois in the Far West." Article in Spring 1963 issue of *Montana: The Magazine of Western History.* The story of the Iroquois Indians who came west with the fur trade and settled among the Bitterroot Salish Indians.
paperback, periodical issue, 8.5 x 10, $3.00

Michael Harrison, "Chief Charlot's Battle with Bureaucracy." Article in Autumn 1960 issue of *Montana: The Magazine of Western History.* Chief Charlot's battle with the federal government to preserve his Salish Indian band in the Bitterroot Valley.
paperback, periodical issue, 8.5 x 10, $3.00

John Kidder, "Montana Miracle: It Saved the Buffalo." Article in Spring 1965 issue of *Montana: The Magazine of Western History.* The importance of the Pablo-Allard buffalo herd on the Flathead Reservation in saving the buffalo from extinction.
paperback, periodical issue, 8.5 x 10, $3.00

Order from:

SKC Press, Box 117, Pablo, MT 59855

Prepayment required on orders from individuals.

Please add shipping charges of $2.00 for first book plus $ .50 for each additional book.

Dedication

To my elders for all the memories and stories they shared. They made our culture come alive.

Our culture is a living experience far beyond what we can record in a book. May Creator help me to pass this knowledge on to today's young people.

Johnny Arlee

Table of Contents

Illustration Credits

Salish Culture Committee, St. Ignatius, Montana
      Eneas and Isabella Granjo photograph
      Blind Mose Chouteh photograph
      John Peter Paul in sweater photograph
      Tony Sandoval drawings
Photograph Archives, Montana Historical Society, Helena, Montana
      Rex C. Haight photographs
Corky Clairmont, Ronan, Montana
      Salish Indian celebration dancers drawings
      Johnny Arlee portrait drawing
      Snake Dance drawing
Johnny Arlee, Arlee, Montana
      Johnny Arlee about 1950 photograph
      Pete Beaverhead photograph
Chris Roberts, Missoula, Montana
      John Peter Paul in headdress photograph
      Louie Plant photograph
George Price, Ravalli, Montana
      Oshanee Kenmille photograph
Char Koosta News, Pablo, Montana
      Johnny and Joan Arlee photograph
Confederated Salish and Kootenai Tribes, Pablo, Montana
      Josh Pepion drawing
Doug Allard, St. Ignatius, Montana
      Mary Finley photograph
Dolly Linsebigler, St. Ignatius, Montana
      Dolly Linsebigler photograph
Jack Brazill, Arlee, Montana
      Bryan Brazill photograph
Louise Combs, Arlee, Montana
      Louise Combs photograph
Kathryn Fehlig, Montana Historical Society, Helena, Montana
      Flathead Reservation map

Editor's Acknowledgments

Many people have generously contributed to this book. Corky Clairmont suggested the original idea and furnished a series of drawings and ideas. Martha Kohl of the Montana Historical Society Press had many valuable suggestions that greatly improved the final product. Johnny Arlee provided his writings, photographs, and knowledge.

All of the employees at the Salish Culture Committee, St. Ignatius, Montana, gave special help in the development of the book. Tony Incashola, director, gave permission to use the Culture Committee's taped interviews, pictures, and drawings. Lucy Vanderburg and Felicite McDonald provided Salish language expertise and helped with many of the identifications of the people photographed at the 1940 Arlee Celebration. Lucy was very patient with my questions about Salish translations. Marie Torosian provided access and guidance in the use of the Culture Committee's photograph collection. Tom Smith helped locate the tape recorded interviews relating to the powwow.

A special thanks is due for the patience and support of all those who agreed to be interviewed about the Salish celebration and/or donated photographs. Your willingness to share your views and knowledge made this book possible.

The SKC Media Center crew—Frank Tyro and Roy Bigcrane—graciously put up with my being underfoot while using the Media Center computers. Al Anderson kindly answered all my stupid computer questions. Jim Ereaux developed the Salish language font used to write the Salish words in this book.

I owe much to all those who read the manuscript for corrections: Allen Hibbard, Mike Dolson, Frank Tyro, and Albert Plant, Jr., of Salish Kootenai College; Delphine Plant of Arlee; Rene Roullier of Ronan; and Scott Bear Don't Walk of Missoula. The Montana Historical Society Press staff found many errors thanks to their careful reading of the manuscript.

All the above and many others have worked to improve the quality of this book. Any surviving mistakes are the sole responsibility of the editor. Please accept my apologies for those mistakes and weaknesses that remain.

Bob Bigart
Pablo, Montana

Over a Century of Moving to the Drum

Editor's Introduction

The Flathead Indian Reservation in western Montana is home to four Salish tribes and one Kootenai tribe. The Salish community of the reservation includes the Bitterroot Valley Salish or Flathead tribe, the Upper Pend d'Oreilles tribe, part of the Lower Pend d'Oreilles tribe, and part of the Spokane tribe. These tribes originally lived in the Upper Columbia River area now covered by western Montana, northern Idaho, and northeastern Washington.

Originally supporting themselves by hunting, fishing, and gathering wild plants, the Salish now hold many jobs in the western Montana economy. They lived for centuries in wealth and comfort based on their knowledge of the plants and animals of the Northern Rockies and, especially, the buffalo of the Great Plains. In the 1990s, Salish people work as teachers, loggers, administrators, politicians, ranchers, clerks, cooks, laborers, and in many other occupations. The tribal economy has changed and diversified, but the community is still strong.

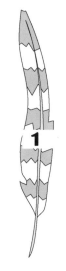

Early in the twentieth century, the tribes were forced to sell most of their land to white homesteaders at bargain prices. The government coerced the tribes to give up the land, and the tribes' income declined and many tribal members were reduced to poverty. At the end of the twentieth century, the Confederated Salish and Kootenai Tribes are still struggling to repair the social and economic damage caused by the opening of the reservation.

Much remains to be done, but the young people in the tribes are showing an increasing interest in preserving the tribes and their traditional tribal culture and values. An especially vibrant, changing, and adapting expression of Salish traditions and values has been the powwow or celebration. For a growing number of Salish people, the celebration is an expression of their Indian identity. The demand for Indian art and

1

craft items for use by dancers at the celebration has encouraged many young people to learn traditional crafts and provides an important market for Salish artisans.

In the 1990s, powwows are held on reservations and in cities all over North America. They are a highlight of the summer for many Indian people and one important way Indian people strengthen and reinforce their tribal communities and share resources and friendship with Indians from other tribes. Celebrations are also important to many Indian families, as they offer a positive drug- and alcohol-free activity for Indian young people.

The Arlee Celebration, like most powwows, includes Indian dancing of various styles. Each session begins with a grand entry or parade of flags, followed by all the dancers grouped by category. A special song is sung in honor of the flags, and a prayer completes the opening ceremonies. The third chapter of this book lists and describes both traditional Salish Indian dances and some new dances borrowed from neighboring tribes. Some of these dances feature special styles of dress. The drawings in chapter three by Corky Clairmont illustrate the different types of dance regalia. Within these general styles, however, each individual's dress reflects the artistic creativity and craftsmanship of the dancer and the artists who created the outfit.

Some of the changes in the traditional powwows include innovations in dance outfits that now spread across Indian country. Western technology, such as sound systems and electric lighting, have also altered the celebrations.

An important aspect of most 1990s powwows, here and across the nation, are the contests. The dancers in each category compete for prize money, and first, second, and third places. As is clear from some of the interviews in this book, the addition of prizes and prize money has changed the celebrations in ways that many Indian people regret because the contests compete with the traditional concept of the powwow as a social function strengthening Salish community values.

Another important aspect of the contemporary powwow is the stick game, a traditional Indian gambling game involving two teams. One team

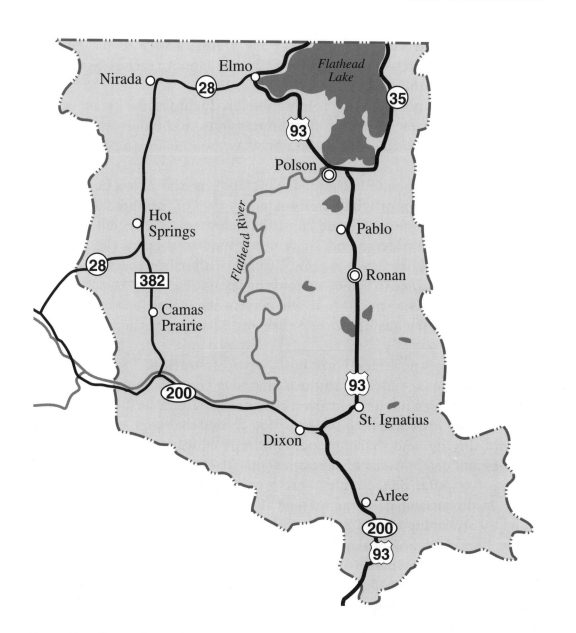

Nirada

Elmo

Flathead Lake

28

35

93

Polson

Flathead River

Hot Springs

Pablo

28

Ronan

382

Camas Prairie

93

200

St. Ignatius

Dixon

Arlee

200

93

3

The Flathead Indian Reservation of Western Montana

hides a marked bone and an unmarked bone. If the other side cannot guess which hand has the unmarked bone, it loses a stick. If the guess is correct, the side guessing gets the bones and a chance to earn sticks. When one side gets all the sticks, they win.

The contemporary Arlee Celebration also includes blackjack, poker, and other card games; various craft concessions; and food stands. Many of those in attendance camp at the powwow grounds for the duration of the celebration.

Today the Arlee Celebration is operated by the Arlee Celebration Committee, which is officially designated by the Confederated Salish and Kootenai Tribes to organize and run the celebration. The members of the committee are volunteers and work year-round to prepare the grounds and to raise money for the powwow. Visitors of all tribes, races, and backgrounds are welcome to come and join the festivities. The Arlee Fourth of July Celebration is a special time when everyone is welcome to share the hospitality and friendship of the Salish and Kootenai Nation.

The Origins of the Arlee Fourth of July Celebration

Celebrations, dancing, and feasting have been an important part of Salish community life for centuries. Historic sources describe tribal camp life involving daily socializing via visiting around the camp, evening dancing and singing, and sharing food, children's education, and craft work. Parades and celebrations of special events, often called War Dances after the most popular dance style, were a regular feature of camp life. The early Jesuit missionaries encouraged the continuation of these celebrations by arranging events based on the many saints' days and holy days in the Roman Catholic calendar.

The earliest evidence of an attempt to hold a Fourth of July Powwow was in 1891. In the 1890s, however, traditional Indian dances were illegal under Bureau of Indian Affairs rules, and the Indian police and Flathead Indian Agent Peter Ronan used the threat of U.S. Army intervention to break up the dance. The Bureau of Indian Affairs found it difficult to argue that it should be illegal to celebrate the Fourth of July, though for a time government attempts to suppress traditional dances forced the tribes to hold them secretly. Because of this persecution, we cannot, at this time, establish definitively when the first Arlee Fourth of July Powwow was held.

The earliest contemporary record is an article in a Missoula newspaper describing the 1900 Fourth of July Powwow or Celebration. In 1977 Blind Mose Chouteh, a Salish elder, placed the first Arlee powwow three years before the 1901 smallpox epidemic. That would put the first Fourth of July Celebration in 1898. Morton J. Elrod, a professor from Missoula and one of the earliest white visitors to the powwow, left some stories about his visit to Indian dances on the Flathead Reservation during the late 1890s. Elrod did not give an exact year or time of year. In 1898 Father George de la Motte, S.J., preached a sermon at Jocko Agency near Arlee that talked about the revelry of the Jocko Indians on July 4, 1898. While the sermon did not mention traditional dances or label the occasion a powwow, presumably de la Motte was preaching against the Fourth of July Powwow, whose significance to the Salish people is celebrated in this book.

Over a Century of Moving to the Drum begins with Johnny Arlee's description of the dances and activities at early Salish celebrations, based on his interviews with Salish elders during the 1970s when he served as the first director of the Salish Culture Committee.

In the second chapter, Arlee recounts some of the changes in the celebrations during his lifetime and shares his views about the value and importance of contemporary Salish Indian celebrations.

The third chapter combines Arlee's descriptions of traditional and borrowed dances at Salish Indian celebrations with Corky Clairmont's drawings of the different styles of outfits worn by the dancers.

The fourth chapter is a photographic essay of an Arlee Fourth of July Celebration held about 1940. The photographer, Rex C. Haight of Missoula, captured the dances and stick games and also documented some of the social aspects of the celebration and camp life.

The fifth, and final, chapter is a collection of interviews about various aspects of Salish celebrations. The first three interviews with Pete Beaverhead, Blind Mose Chouteh, and Mary Finley were taken from the Salish Culture Committee's tapes of interviews recorded in the 1970s.

In two of these interviews, Salish elder Pete Beaverhead related in the 1970s that Sam Resurrection, a Salish leader in the early twentieth century, brought the War Dance to the Flathead Reservation from the Cheyenne Indians. The Salish had War Dances and celebrations for many years before the 1890s, so it is unclear exactly what Pete Beaverhead meant. Possibly Sam Resurrection brought a new style of War Dance from the Cheyennes in the late 1890s.

6

Please note that the selections from the Salish Culture Committee tapes used in this book have been translated from Salish to English and modified from an oral to a written format. Every effort has been made to keep the meaning of the original Salish, but the selections have been edited for English grammar and clarity. They are not word for word translations from the Salish. The original tapes are available at the Salish Culture Committee, St. Ignatius, Montana.

Other interviews with John Peter Paul, the present Salish War Dance Chief; Dolly Linsebigler; Oshanee Kenmille; and Louise Combs touch on a variety of memories and views about the Arlee celebration. The last two interviews with Bryan Brazill and Louie Plant sample the views of two young Salish powwow dancers.

Sources on the Origins of the Arlee Powwow

Peter Ronan to Commissioner of Indian Affairs, July 1, 1891, #24,117/1891, letters received, RG 75, Records of the Commissioner of Indian Affairs, National Archives, Washington, D.C.

"Indian Celebration: Fourth of July Observed by the Flatheads at Arlee," *Edward's Fruit Grower & Farmer* (Missoula, MT) July 13, 1900, page 6, col. 2.

Interview with Blind Mose Chouteh, Feb. 15, 1977, tape 96, side 1, Salish Culture Committee Oral History & Culture Archives, St. Ignatius, MT.

"Indian Boys Are Like Other Boys," box 14, folder 13, MS UM4, Morton J. Elrod Papers, K. Ross Toole Archives, Mansfield Library, University of Montana, Missoula, MT.

Father George de la Motte, S.J., "A Dream of Mine: July 4, 1898, in the Midst of My Indians' Revelry." Tape recording of English translation of Salish language sermon translated by Robert Sherwood in 1982, personal collection of Johnny Arlee, Arlee, MT. The original manuscript, written in Salish, is at Sacred Heart Mission, DeSmet, ID.

Interviews with Pete Beaverhead, Feb. 28, 1975, tape 18, side 2; and Mar. 14. 1975, tape 35, side 1, Salish Culture Committee Oral History & Culture Archives, St. Ignatius, MT.

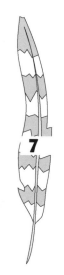

drawing by Josh Pepion

Yamncut łu Sqelixʷ
The Gathering of the People
by Johnny Arlee

"Well, I remember an elder telling about the good old days. The leaders would gather at a home. They would fill their pipe, smoke, and then begin their meeting. Different ones in the group would get up and speak towards the celebration. One person would pull out his money pouch and donate $50.00; then another person donated money; then a couple of richer Indians stood up and donated money plus a cow. The Indians donated a lot of money. Maybe hundreds of dollars were collected. This was used to buy food for the celebration. They bought coffee, sugar, salt, baking powder, flour, and such. The cost of food a long time ago was cheap. You could buy 100 pounds of sugar for $3.75 and 50 pounds of flour for $.90. Today, it isn't that way, everything is expensive. The cows that were donated were left with a caretaker until the celebration started. These cows would be butchered to be given out to the encampment. Different ones in the group were given duties for the celebration: one person to take care of the cows, one to handle the money to buy the rations, others to maintain the war dance pavilion, some to cut tipi poles, and some to be camp criers. There would be some who would come late to the meeting, and they would be filled in on what had been discussed.

"The place and location of the celebration was chosen—a place where there was good water, plenty of grass for the horses, lots of good firewood, and level ground. They would figure out how many days they were going to celebrate. Then the messengers were sent out in different directions to deliver the news of the upcoming celebration.

"After, when the local businesses heard of the celebration, they also donated money or goods. Many of them were thankful because the celebration also benefited them. One time we had some cows left over from the celebration. They were left with the caretaker until the next year's powwow."
—*Salish Celebration Pageant manuscript*

Campers Day

The camp was set up by the family. Grandmother directed each member of the family in the tipi setup. Grandfather, Father, and Son tied the four main poles and stood them up. Then the rest of the poles were placed in position as directed by Grandmother. Mother and Daughter took the tipi out of the bag, unfolded it, and tied it to a special pole. Then, with Father helping, they stood and positioned the special pole in place. Grandfather and Son unloaded the bag with the pegs and pins, and took them out.

10

Grandmother, with Daughter helping her, took one side of the tipi and Father and Mother took the other side of the tipi. Grandmother was still giving instructions. They covered the tipi poles and adjusted the tipi flaps. Father lifted Son up to place the tent pins to connect the tipi flaps together. Grandfather, Mother, and Daughter went inside the tipi to push the poles out and tighten the tipi. Grandmother was still giving instructions on which pole to move. Son pounded pegs into the ground to tighten down the tipi. Father and Grandfather placed the ear poles. Grandmother stood back, looked at the camp setup, and gave her final approval. Then the bundles were taken off the wagon and into the tipi.

The children were anxious to go and play and visit their friends. Before they were allowed to go play, Grandmother instructed the children about Camper's Day. The law was that the children were not to be running about and hollering or hooping around. This was to show respect for the people who had Memorial Keepsakes. All the children were taught this, even the older boys and girls. Then the children were turned loose to visit and play very quietly. Some men drove a wagon around with the rations for the encampment.

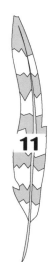

11

Memorial Parade

The first morning, after the camps were set up, the leaders gathered at the Chief's camp. The Chief discussed the day's activities. After it was clear what was to happen, the Camp Crier went out to make his announcements to the encampment.

The Camp Crier rode his horse around the campground saying, "Can I have your attention. My fellow people, today, after you've had breakfast, you will get ready. You that have Memorial Keepsakes—the horses of your loved ones, the clothing of your loved ones—you will get them ready. You will bring these out to be shown to the people. If it's been one year, or two years, that you've had these keepsakes, this is the time. You will bring these out. There will be someone coming around to let you know where to gather, and who will lead you."

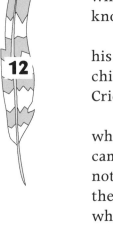

The Camp Crier continued riding around the campground repeating his message. The children followed behind the Camp Crier. Some of the children ran off to their own camps to relay the message of the Camp Crier.

Shortly after the Camp Crier had passed by, there was another man who was walking to each camp's doorway and asked if anyone in this camp had Memorial Keepsakes to show. If not, he went on to the next camp and asked the same question. If so, then he told them where to go and gather with the rest of the group to get ready.

In the old times when someone passed away, the survivors looked among the people and found a person who resembled the deceased and was like that person in every respect. The family then gave the deceased's belongings to this certain person. They never divided up the clothing.

One man was put in charge as the leader of the Memorial Parade Group. After the people got themselves ready, the leader led the group into camp, shouting aloud, and talking about the Memorial Keepsakes of the people. The encampment began to cry in memory of their loved ones.

The procession did not go fast, just a walking pace, all in single file. First came the men, dressed in the Indian clothing of the loved ones. Then came the horses with all the decorations. The Memorial Procession went around the encampment two times. While they were going around, the group sang the Memorial Songs [es nunše].

During the mourning period, the widowed person remained at home for a period of one year. The widow or widower put on his or her poorest clothing. Their hair was never combed, their face never painted, and they avoided ornaments.

The bereaved person had an old man or woman cut the mourner's hair almost to the scalp. One factor deciding the length of the mourning period was the growth of the mane and tail of the deceased's favorite horse. These were cut off as close as the mourner's hair. This horse was never worked. Nor was it taken east on the Plains. It was left in the care of some relatives.

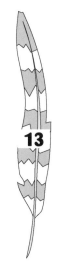

The widowed person went to live with the parents-in-law for the whole mourning period. This was done primarily to be near them to comfort them in their sorrow. Since all or most of the household goods had been distributed at the feast, the bereaved had literally lost house and home by giving their property away. When the parents-in-law considered the time of mourning long enough, they presented the person with a fine outfit of clothing. This formally released the mourner from all obligations and gave the parents-in-law's consent to remarriage. The new mate was often a brother or sister of the former spouse. When the man or woman suddenly emerged from the lodge clean, well-groomed, and dressed in the best clothing available, it was known that the mourning period was over.

13

Celebration Time Begins

Shortly after those in the Memorial Procession returned to their camps, the Chief circled the encampment on horseback saying, "It is now time that we turn ourselves loose. All of you, my people, change your clothes, comb your hair, everybody get ready. You men and women, all of you children, let us be happy. Let's hoop and holler. Now we begin our celebration. After you have had lunch then we will begin our War Dance and celebration."

Shortly after the Chief passed by with his announcement, the Camp Crier rode slowly by saying, "Can I have your attention, all of you my people. Now we get ready—all of us—to celebrate. We have shed our tears for our loved ones. We will celebrate today and the next few days. We dance the dances of our ancestors. Everyone, do your best. Don't be ashamed. Don't be hesitant. Don't get mad. All of you men and women, all of you young and old, you beautiful and ugly, let us all be happy. Get your horses ready. Get yourselves dressed and ready. Ride throughout the camp. You drummers and singers get ready. We're going to dance this afternoon. All you women begin cooking."

Soon from all over the camp, the smoke filled the air. It wasn't long after the people finished eating that the Camp Crier circled the encampment calling for the dancers and drummers to get ready.

Before the dancing began, a procession formed outside of the camp circle to the north and entered from the east. Many of the people were mounted, and the riders and horses were decked in the finest possible attire. Sometimes the men formed in one line and the women in another. At other times, the men rode ahead and the women and children behind. The people rode four circles sunwise [south, west, north, and east] around the inside of the camp circle, each time going at a faster gait. At last the men broke into a fast lope towards the dance arena. The women followed and struck their hands against their lips making a quivering call, "li li li li li li li li." At the arena, the men jumped off their horses and rushed in and began to dance while the women and boys took charge of their horses. This parade was called the čm̓šm̓šte.

Snake Dance

The dancers gathered to the north outside of the campsite. The Snake Dance began from this direction. The leader led the group to the east, outside of camp, and then entered the camp circle dancing towards the dance pavilion in the center of the camp. The pattern of the dance was made in a serpentine fashion. They danced in a circle against the sun [south, east, north, and west] and then advanced west some distance and danced another circle. In this way, they danced in four circles before reaching the dance pavilion. They entered it through the east entrance. The leader danced around sunwise in the dance arena with the group following. He kept dancing around towards the middle to form a coil like a snake. By this time, the drummers and singers were approaching the dance area. They had followed the Snake Dance group, escorting them with song.

It was said that the Snake Dance represented a group of warriors returning from a raiding party from the north. They entered the camp through the east tired and weak from their journey. They performed this dance of the snake.

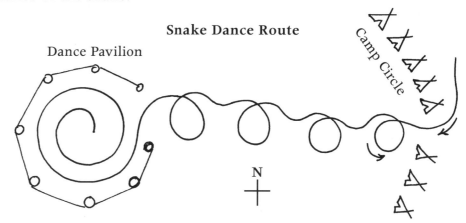

Snake Dance Route

Dance Pavilion

Camp Circle

N

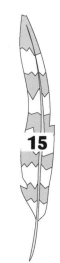

War Dancing

The War Dancing began with drummers and singers seated at the west end of the dance pavilion. The Dance Chief stood to the east and

carried a ceremonial whip. The dancers sat or squatted on the outer edge of the dancing area. The spectators were behind them and the drummers on the outside. When the music started, the Chief went around the circle of dancers, following the sun's course, with a hopping step, flourishing his whip and calling, "xᵂu, xᵂa" [start or go]. He tapped or gently whipped many of the dancers as he passed along. They immediately rose, passed into the dancing area, and began to dance. The Dance Chief danced counter to the other dancers, passing around them, and sometimes in and out through them, encouraging them. The earliest way of dancing was for all the dancers to dance counter-sunwise in a circle. The music stopped, and, after a short rest, the singers began another song. The Chief rose and went around, urging the men with his whip as before.

In the old style of War Dance, all carried weapons. The dancers danced making motions as if looking for an enemy, looking for tracks, scanning the horizon, attacking an enemy, stabbing with spears, or striking with tomahawks. The dancers dressed in their best clothes and best war bonnets. Some had only moccasins, breechcloth, and headdress. Their faces were painted and hair done up as for war. The red paint [yučmn] was the mark of blood, indicating the person had done battle with the enemy. Red marks on his horse indicated it also had done battle. Stripes of red, yellow, and black were common. The legs were often painted yellow or white. Putting on paint was also a prayer that neither his blood, nor the blood of his horse, would be spilled.

In the old style War Dance, many kinds of headdresses were used. In addition to the common war bonnets made of eagle tail feathers, headdresses were also made of entire skins of birds, head skins of animals, or set with buffalo, antelope, or deer horns. War Dances were done when war was anticipated, before going to war, before going on a raid, before making an attack, or when expecting to be attacked.

Evening Ride Songs

The Evening Ride was a social event of no ritual or official significance. The men rode around the camp circle singing the songs, and the women stood around singing them also. The woman chose a man she wanted to ride with, and the man held his foot out stiff so the woman could use his foot to jump up behind him. Not only unmarried women, but married women also might do this. It was considered sport. The women were dressed in their good clothes. Sometimes a woman might tease her husband by jumping on somebody else's horse. It was lots of fun.

17

Canvas Dancing

The Canvas Dance songs were sung to say farewell to the people and to recruit other individuals to journey into enemy territory to gain honor in war, raiding, or stealing horses. One man began to sing from camp to camp, and soon he was joined in the singing by others. The group carried a buffalo robe or hides sewn together and used sticks to pound on the hide in tune with the song.

The individual who had decided to go on a war or raiding party began singing and pounding on the robe. As others joined him in the singing, they were pledging themselves to join him on his journey. The men sang while walking from camp to camp in a counter-sunwise direction. The women walked and sang behind their husbands. The women's song was for their husbands to come home safely. At the end of the dance, the women went back to the tipi, and the men left camp.

The raiders left after they had gone once around the camp circle. Those who were staying behind might go around the circle again. The raiding party was supposed to leave camp secretly, before daylight, while the dance was still in progress. They would travel all day, and that night the leader told the party when they could rest.

Some younger warriors went along with the group, maybe even one going on his first raiding party. The boy's mother put many pairs of moccasins in his bag for his journey. The young lad on his first raiding party was pitiful. The warriors in the party sat waiting for him to serve them a drink of water. There was a certain cup to drink from, made from a buffalo horn. It was called q̓muʔlamn. The horn was tied with buckskin that looped over the shoulder.

18

The leader said to this young novice, "Go bring me some water to drink." The water would be quite a distance from the group, but the lad did as he was told. He brought water for the leader to drink. After the leader drank, he told the young man to spill the water. Then the lad had to get water for each warrior in this same fashion, spilling the water after each one drank. The novice was being taught to be a good warrior.

After the raiding party met the enemy and the young man returned home leading a horse, it was as if he had come alive. When they returned to camp, the leader reported on the young warrior. He described the lad's deeds to the Chief and explained how well things had turned out for him.

The Chief asked, "Did you steal?"

The lad answered proudly, "Yes."

Then the Chief told him, "The next time you go along on a raiding party, don't get water for anyone. You will have your own cup to drink from. And whoever the next lad will be will bring you water to drink. When the leaders or Chiefs have a meeting, they will call you to join them because you've been recognized as a warrior. Get a good straight stick and whittle it until the stick is clean and smooth. Then mark it with red and tie an eagle feather to it. This will be your coup stick and the stripe will indicate the one horse you have stolen. Also, mark your blanket with a red stripe."

When the young warrior was out on his next raiding party, he might kill one or two of his enemy during battle. This was corroborated by his companions when they returned home. The Chief told him to mark his stick and blanket again. He marked these until he had many stripes to show his rank. It took many great deeds and many years to earn the right to carry the Indian flag and become next in line to be a leader or Chief.

During a battle, the one who carried the Indian flag was the leader of the war party. He did not run away. He jumped forward and then lay down and stuck the flag in the ground. As he advanced, the war party followed. If he happened to get wounded or killed and dropped the flag, the next in line to become leader picked up the flag and advanced. The Indian flag was called sčcḭa.

The Indian shield called šᴧ̣e was carried by the person who was next in line to become leader. He had already proven himself as brave and smart and had been in battles. During the battle with the enemy, when they were still some distance away, this man would ride towards the enemy line holding his shield. He waved it around so that he did not get hit by the enemy fire. He rode back and forth in front of the enemy line until his leader called him back. He gained honor and earned stripes and feathers.

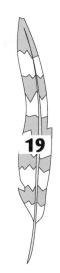

At any gathering, a warrior's rank was determined by his deeds of honor. These were enumerated by the decorations on the symbolic or ceremonial objects he carried. These objects included sticks with a crooked end, spears decorated with eagle feathers, short sticks with decorated hoops at the end, decorated clubs, quirts, rattles, pipes, and especially decorated sashes, arm bands, head bands, and garters. Certain men carried no weapons of offense or defense. These were the Fearless Men who could go into the thick of battle and come out uninjured.

The Golden Eagle was the protector of the Indian people. His feathers were signs of leadership when worn on bonnets or tied on Indian flags, shields, tipis, lances, horses, etc.

19

Wake-up Song

During the early morning, a singing group would circle the encampment sunwise going from camp to camp. There was just one song that was sung for this occasion. This was the Wake-up Song. A dancer accompanied the group of singers. This dancer approached a tipi and, if the door flap was still closed, the dancer entered the tipi and danced a complete circle before leaving. The dancer did not shake anyone awake. The Wake-up Group then proceeded to the next camp. If there was a person standing at the door of the tipi, then the Wake-up Group passed by to another camp while continuing with the song. They sang from camp to camp until the group completed the full circle of the encampment.

The early morning Wake-up Group was more or less telling you, "It is time to wake up, because you are celebrating. You can sleep when you get home." In those times, they didn't go into the tipi and pull the blankets off the people. They woke them up in a respectful manner. They also told the campers if there were warriors out on a raiding party, so the people could keep the raiding party in mind to prayerfully support the group.

Early in the morning after the Wake-up Song, the Camp Crier rode around the complete circle of camps calling for all the Chiefs and leaders to gather at the Head Chief's tipi to plan the events for that day. After the meeting, the Camp Crier rode around the encampment again, announcing the activities to be performed during that day and evening.

The War Dancing began as early as 10 a.m. Everyone was lighthearted and happy. In later years after alcohol was introduced to the Indians, some of the men and even some women would be found inebriated. There weren't any jails. The Chief's Police Society tied the offenders to wagon wheels.

Sometimes about 2 or 3 p.m., there would be someone tied to a wagon wheel for the public to view. In many cases after being tied to a wagon wheel a few times, the embarrassment caused the offender to be more careful in the future.

There was a blind man at the early Salish celebrations who was always tied to a wagon wheel for being drunk. He sold his whiskey by the drink. He took an empty pint, filled his mouth from his whiskey bottle, and then spit into the empty pint the number of drinks for which the buyer asked.

There was another dance which was called the Prairie Chicken Dance, snxʷalmncutn. This dance was brought to the people by a man who had journeyed to the prairies. One day while he was resting, he heard some singing. He carefully looked over the tall grass and saw the prairie chickens rolling in the dust and shaking themselves off and dancing. When the man returned to the camp, he showed this dance to the people.

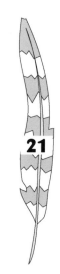

21

Sham Battle

One of the highlights of the early powwows was the enactment of the sham battle. While the War Dancing was going on, the scout returned to the village with news. He didn't ride straight into camp, but rode his horse in a zigzag fashion. He wore a red blanket caped over his shoulders and tied or pinned in the front of the neck. The scout howled like a wolf. When someone heard the scout approaching, that person cried out to the people in the camp, "Qe hewšiłlt, qe hewšiłlt." [We are being barked at.] "Everyone come." The bells of the dancers rang as everyone went to see the approaching scout. At the edge of camp the Chief spread out a blanket on the ground and stood behind the blanket facing the oncoming scout. The Chief held a stick in his hand. The people were behind the Chief standing side by side, two or three rows deep. They started singing the song to greet the scout, snhewmi. The people swayed from side to side in rhythm with the song.

The scout was still riding his horse in a zigzag motion. The scout stooped over on his horse as if he were lying down. The horse galloped slowly, and the scout groaned or howled like a wolf, "Huuuuuuuu."

Someone from the group shouted war cries. The scout approached the blanket, and the Chief hit him lightly with the stick. The scout was in a trance. Then the scout shouted out "Ye$^{?}$," which meant he saw human beings, or "X^{w}i$^{?}$," which meant he saw buffalo.

22

"Ye$^{?}$," the Chief would say. "$^{?}$a, ye$^{?}$, you have been scouting, but are in a trance and don't even see or know your own path. Okay tell us your news."

The group of people stopped singing when the Chief hit the scout with the stick. Then the scout reported what he had seen. "Over there, there are six people. I don't know what tribe they are. They are near the horses that are standing over there by the creek. They are crawling towards the horses, and they are carrying something on their backs."

When the celebration was being planned, a meeting was set up with those warriors who had been on raiding parties. They gathered the ones who were smart and had good memories. They were told that they were going to reenact a battle scene. So the warriors worked together to select the battle tactics they had used in a certain encounter with the enemy. They planned together what they were going to do. Then they began their mock battle after the Dog Scout brought the news that he had sighted the enemy invaders.

The warriors cried, "X^{w}ux^{w}a." Their faces were painted. They mounted their horses, and some rode double. At the rear of the group followed the

Dog or Dog Scout on foot. Within a short distance of the enemy, the leader of the warriors stopped and sang the Dog's Song. After the song he shouted the Dog's name, "Kᵂlaw, k̓ᵂlaw, k̓ᵂlaw, k̓ᵂlaw."

Then the Dog was heard calling, "Wiu, wiu, wiu, wiu," as he went to the front of the warriors where the leader stood.

"Kᵂlaw, k̓ᵂlaw, go this way to where the enemy is," the leader said.

The Dog went toward the enemy barking, "We, we, we."

The Dog's relatives might give him a horse and a rifle or six gun to arm himself with and kill many of the enemy. Many times the Dog went into the midst of the enemy without any weapons. He rode around the enemy to humiliate them. The Dog's power was great. The enemy couldn't catch him, kill him, or harm him. If there were two Dogs sent into battle, they would kill many enemies. That's how powerful they were. Then, if the Dog were not stopped or chased back, he kept going until the enemy killed him.

There weren't any Dog Societies. This was an individual role through the guardian spirit of the dog. The spirit gave the warrior the strength to be brave and fierce. He was given directions on how to arm himself. Sometimes he carried only a shield or only a knife. But he always carried a rattle made of rawhide filled with rocks which was called c̓ale.

If the Dog was a family man, his family wouldn't want him to leave. The wife grabbed the bridle of his horse to turn him back to camp. He might get turned aside on the first try, but he tried again until he succeeded in going.

The warriors attacked the enemy, singing the Battle Song [esotenši], shooting and making war cries. There were also some women who went

23

among the men warriors in battle. These women were the brave and fearless ones. They were called šinm̓sčin.

During one of the mock battles, a man was leading his horses from his camp to the creek to be tied where there was good grass and plenty of water. He was a latecomer to the celebration and had just finished setting up camp. The warriors in the mock battle took his horses, all in fun. They returned the horses to him after the mock battle.

By the time the battle ended, many scalps were taken. Also horses or even a girl might be captured. Upon nearing the camp, the victorious warriors halted at a distance in order to decorate themselves for a triumphant entry. Those who had counted coup blackened their faces with charcoal to indicate their victory over the enemy. They all dressed in their finest outfits and feathered bonnets. Then the victory party rode towards the camp singing the victory song. The scalps taken were tied on the end of a long stick and carried by a warrior at the head of the victory party. He rode back and forth in front of the group. This was called esčinme. He gave war cries. The victory party followed, riding side by side, spread out in rows. Everyone sang and shouted war cries. The party galloped into camp. Each warrior who had gained honors moved his horse from side to side. This was an attempt to prevent the old people from halting him by grasping the bridle of his horse. Those old people who succeeded in grasping the bridle were presented with a stick. The stick represented the gift of a captured horse. The recipient then expressed his or her gratitude and honored the warrior by singing a Praise or Glad Song, "Lemti qʷelm."

24

One old lady might come out of camp shouting, "Give me that scalp." When she received the scalp, she chewed it and shouted, "You must be the one who killed my man, my boy," or whomever she had lost. Then another lady took the scalp and chewed on it and passed the scalp on to yet another lady who wiped her butt on it.

The victory party rode through the camp and made two complete circles of the encampment. Then the women prepared for the next day's activity, the Scalp Dance.

Borrowing Wives

The next day, in the morning, a man walked around the encampment singing a song. He was borrowing women for the Scalp Dance [esk̓ʷułni t noxʷnxʷ]. He said, "Loan me your wife. We're going to scalp dance, ah. Loan me your daughter. We're going to Scalp Dance, ah he, yo he yo. Loan me you qeneʔ [paternal grandmother]. We're going to Scalp Dance, hey. Loan me your čč̓yeʔ [maternal grandmother]. We're going to Scalp Dance, hey. Ah he, yo, he yo." Then the women who were to participate in the Scalp Dancing followed the man. There were many women, and they went to the tipis where those preparing for the Scalp Dance gathered.

At the camps where the ceremony of dressing and painting the faces of the Scalp Dancers was to take place, the men brought men's clothing, bonnets, scalps, etc. The items the warriors had used during battle were now to be worn by the Scalp Dancers. The song for preparing the Scalp Dancers was called esq̓ey̓snwe [they are painting one another's faces]. The women didn't choose how to be painted or dressed. The designated men painted the women's faces, fixed their hair, and selected a headdress to wear. The women were told which tipi they were to enter to be prepared. Sometimes they didn't want to go to one tipi because the man there didn't do a very good job painting their faces, but they couldn't refuse. After the women were finished, their husbands

25

and family couldn't recognize them. The song for preparing the Scalp Dancers was sung until the women were ready. A man would ask if they were finished. When they were, each group was escorted to the dance pavilion.

The first group was escorted to the dance arena. There was a song sung while they paraded to the pavilion. When the group entered the dance arena, they made one complete circle and then went to the center and waited for the other groups to arrive.

When all the Scalp Dancers had arrived at the dance pavilion, the drummers lined up side by side, drumming on hand drums in the center of the arena. They were not dressed in fancy clothing. The women formed a circle dancing side by side, facing inward, and moving sunwise. The step was a little different from the Round Dance, more like a Jumping Dance. The songs of the Scalp Dance were many. One song the adults sang was more or less stolen or borrowed from the young boys and girls. This song was called "Tiwene? Husband." The children were about thirteen or fourteen years old. One of them, the eldest from the group, walked with a limp. His name was Tiwene?. He liked to enjoy himself and joined in when the children played. The young girls were always teasing each other about having Tiwene? as a husband. This song was made up by the young boys and girls. The adults liked it so they sang it during the Scalp Dancing.

26

Before the people realized it, a few of the women Scalp Dancers were gone from the dance. When they returned, they were led by a man. Their faces were painted black with charcoal. They wore dresses of old gunny sacks or old hides with sunflower leaves, bushes, and bones or shells tied to them. These women were the brave and fearless ones. They went to battle with the men and rode in front of the enemy lines, giving shrill war cries and never being shot. No one recognized them. The Scalp Dancers formed a long row, standing side by side, and facing the men who were already formed in a row. The song for the warrior women was sung. The Scalp Dancers danced toward the drummers and stopped in front of them. Then they danced backwards to their original starting point, and then forward again. After the song had been sung for four starts or verses, these brave and fearless women went among the drummers. The dancers teased the drummers by gathering around one of the men. A dancer placed the stick with the scalp tied on the end over the drummer's shoulder. If the man didn't push the stick away from his shoulder, he was automatically married to the woman. That was one of the ways to get married a long time ago. When the song finished, the people played with the warrior women, teasing and chasing them until they eventually left the dance pavilion. Then one final song was sung, and the dance ended. When the women celebrated a victorious battle, they used to do the Scalp Dance for four or five days.

Dog Begging

One day the Dog Scout rode around camp singing his Begging Song. This was called esx̣ƛ́cini [he is feeding or grazing]. The Dog Scout carried a rattle made of rawhide filled with pebbles, called c̓ałe. The rider went from camp to camp, stopping at each camp. The people inside of the tipi gave food; they gave handkerchiefs; they gave blankets; and they tied them on the Dog Scout or his horse. They tied the gifts anywhere: on the man's foot, his hair, around his neck, on the horse's tail, or around the horse's neck. The Dog didn't talk and couldn't refuse anything. The people tried their best to make the Dog smile or laugh. When the Dog got back to his camp, his wife untied the food and gifts he had received. It was as if he were being paid for his services and bravery. He didn't have to hunt or gather roots and berries for he had an important job for the tribe.

27

The Gathering of the Warriors and the Lost Article Dance

One day during the War Dancing, and after the sham battle, there was a ceremony which took place. The song for gathering the old warriors to tell their great deeds, called the qaqiit, was sung. During the singing of this song, there were two designated helpers who went out and escorted the old warriors to the dance pavilion. As each of the chosen warriors were escorted to the dance pavilion by the two helpers, they were met by the dance leader standing at the entrance to the dance arena. The group followed the dance leader once around the arena sunwise and then to the place where the warriors were seated. Then another person was mentioned for the helpers to get and bring into the pavilion. As each of the warriors was escorted around the pavilion, the crowd gave war shrills. The song continued until all the chosen warriors who were to give account of their great deeds were gathered. Then the song ended.

The Lost Article Dance was originally only used as part of the ceremony of the Gathering of the Warriors to tell of their war deeds. Today it is used when an eagle feather is dropped during the dancing to show the special respect Indian people have for the eagle. The Lost Article Dance began with a number of young men squatting or kneeling near the feathers and other items that had been dropped. These were laid out on the ground. The song of the Lost Article was sung, sntiplscu. The dancers formed a circle with the lost articles in the center. The drum began at a fast and rolling beat. All the dancers extended their arms towards the lost articles while kneeling on one knee and shaking the other leg to make the bells ring. They moved their arms holding fans, war clubs, coup sticks, etc. When the drum beat changed to a slower beat, the dancers rose and danced inwards towards the lost items. As they reached the items, the drum beat changed back to the fast rolling rhythm, and all the dancers returned to their original positions, then kneeled, and raised their arms. They went forward and back four times in this way. On the fifth start of the song, the dancers danced sunwise in a circle. One of the young dancers danced counter-sunwise in the middle of the main group around the lost articles. He danced towards the lost items and backed away as the main group of dancers gave war cries shying him away. He did this four times, each time approaching closer to the lost items. The third time he almost touched the lost articles, and the fourth time he picked them up. The music ended with a rolling beat. The dancers gave war cries and walked to the west where the leader was. After presenting the lost articles to the leader, the dancers sat down.

One warrior stood up to recount his war exploits. He planted his ceremonial stick or spear in the ground and placed his hand on the upright spear. Then he recounted the details of each warlike deed, stating whom he had killed, wounded, and counted coup on. He spoke slowly and plainly. He wore only moccasins, breechcloth, necklace, armlets, and headband. His whole body was painted yellow except the right leg below the calf, which was painted red. He explained that he was painted this way because the deeds he narrated took place on the Yellowstone River in a great battle with the Blackfeet.

29

As each warrior stood up to recount his great deeds, he began, "X̌ʷukʷhey čn x̌eyilš." [Okay, I enter to speak. I went on a raiding party.] "I carried a pipe; I stole a horse; I cut something red; I claimed something red." Sounds from the drum and war cries from the crowd followed whatever the warrior mentioned. If the object taken or the act of bravery was great, then the drum beat four times. If the warrior took something small, then the drum would be hit only once. The drum beat one, two, three, or four times, depending on the importance of each warlike deed. At each pause in the account, the drum beat and war cries were given as emphasis or applause. In the center of the arena was a pole in the ground with pegs sticking out like nails. While the warrior told of his great deeds, members of his family brought blankets, shawls, scarves, necklaces, moccasins, beaded bags, etc., to the center pole and hung them on the pole. Money was gathered and tied in a scarf and hung on the pole. All of these collected items were given away to honor the warrior who was recounting his great deeds. The gifts were distributed after he had completed his story. The money gathered by the family was given to the visitors who had traveled a long way.

When the warrior finished recounting his great deeds, he said, "Šehoy" [That's all]. Then the drummers sang the special song for a warrior who had just recounted his great deeds. War cries came from the audience. Then the War Dance leader announced, "Ha yo, you're crazy. What if you had been killed. You shouldn't have done a thing like that. You should be thankful that you're still alive today. If you had done this deed today, you'd be put into the penitentiary."

The War Dances and Social Dances Continue

After the warriors had completed stories of their great war deeds and accomplishments, a couple of War Dance Songs were sung. During the War Dancing, the dancers danced many different dances. There was one dance which was the old time War Dancing done by the old warriors. This was called the snčspl̓q̓mncu. It was described as a dance in which "their chest was kind of downward and their back side kind of upward." The older dance step was more like a hop. They all carried weapons. They danced, making motions as if looking for the enemy, looking for tracks, scanning the horizon, attacking an enemy, stabbing with spears, or aiming their bow and arrows. The sounds of old time War Dancers were that of animals, like the grunting sounds of the buffalo, "wa, wa, wa, wa, x^w, x^w x^w." The dancers were stripped of their clothing. A few only wore breechcloths. Many of the warriors danced with their privates exposed. With the coming of Christianity, this dance was condemned because of its immoral exposure. Today, if you did this dance, you would have to be very brave.

30

Some dancers showed bravery by dancing over crossed swords. The long swords of the calvary soldiers were called čulule. They were filed sharp and laid on the ground crossways with the sharp part of the blade upward. With their moccasins off, the dancers stood with their feet between the crossed swords and another song of the snčsp̓lq̓mncutn began. The dancers began dancing. As the drum beat faster, the dancers kept in time with the music, placing their feet between the crossed blades. When the song concluded, the dancers checked their feet. They proved they were brave warriors because their feet weren't bleeding or cut by the blades of the swords.

During the War Dancing, one song was sung for the Smoking of the Pipe. This was called the sn̓imscu [to catch someone off guard or unaware]. Many times the drummers and singers, in fun, tried to catch the people unaware this song was being sung. After this song, four more War Dance Songs were sung. If no one brought a lit pipe filled with tobacco to the drummers and singers by the end of the fourth War Dance Song, the drummers and singers gave a rolling beat on the drum. This indicated the dance had ended. The people said, "Ha yo, qe tqaq." [On no, we got caught.]

They blamed one another. One said, "Maybe you knew and didn't say anything."

The other person said, "No, I also got caught."

In many cases when the Smoking Song was sung, there was a woman who knew its meaning. She would run around busily looking for a pipe. When she found one, she quickly filled the pipe and lit it for the drummers before the fourth song was completed. Then the dancing continued. The pipe was very sacred for the Indian people. It was used in ceremonies, talks, peace, prayer, etc.

A long time ago, as a sign of peace towards other tribes, one tribe stood side by side in a long row. Each person held one arm upward and forward, with hand open and palm facing the other group. A Song of Peace was sung. The peaceful group slowly walked towards the other group. The other tribes recognized this as a sign of peace. They also formed a

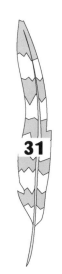

long row, and began singing their Song of Peace and walked slowly to meet the oncoming peaceful group. When the two groups finished their songs, four war cries were given, and then they shook hands. The leaders sat down. The leaders who were extending peace filled a pipe and shared a smoke with the other tribal leaders. Smoking the pipe together was a special pledge of friendship. When they finished with the smoke, the other leaders also offered a smoke. When the leaders finished their smoke for peace, the groups got up and shook hands again. Thus everyone became allies.

There were breaks throughout the War Dancing for some of the social dancing. One such dance was the very popular Owl Dance. In the Owl Dance, usually the woman gets to choose her dancing partner. The drummers and singers moved to the center of the dance arena and stood with one hand holding the large drum off of the ground and the other hand holding the drumstick. The dancers moved in a sunwise direction around a circle. Couples danced together with the men on the outside of the circle and the women on the inside. The man put his right arm around the waist of his partner, and the woman put her left arm around the man's waist. The man's left hand and the woman's right hand were clasped together in front. The step was a shuffle with the dancers placing one foot forward on the half beat of the drum and drawing the other foot forward on the softer half beat. Halfway through the verse of the song, the drummers softened the drum beat drastically. This signaled the couples to turn around once in place and resume their progress around the circle when the drum returned to full volume. No one refused to dance when asked. To say "no" could be costly and embarrassing. The woman had the right to select a part of the man's dance outift as payment for the refusal. Today the penalty is usually five dollars. This dance was said to have been introduced from another tribe in the early 1900s.

Other social dances done during the War Dancing were the Round Dance or Gift Dance. At the end of the fourth War Dance song, the drum beat at a roll and then stopped. This meant that it was the end of that part

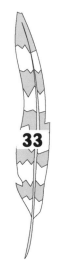

of the songs and a different dance was to be performed. As the Round Dance Song was sung, the dancers went sunwise in a circle. Both men and women danced in no particular order. The drummers and singers were in the middle, and the dancers faced in toward them. The dancers moved sideways with a hitching step. The ones who were going to give gifts made an inner circle, also going sunwise and facing the drummers. When a person was ready, he chose a partner from the outer ring or from the assembled crowd. He and his partner, man or woman, then hooked arms and danced around the inner ring. When the song was finished, the people in the outer circle sat down and the announcer or leader came into the circle and stood near the singers. The announcer selected the person who wanted to give a gift. This person said, "I give this man or woman such and such." Most of the payments were small, such as tobacco, fifty cents, a dollar, a handkerchief, scarf, blanket, shawl, etc. The announcer then held up the article given, walked around the circle showing it to every-body, and said, "For all of you people to know. This person gives this gift to his dance partner. This gift does not belong to the original owner. It now belongs to the chosen dance partner." Then he gave it to the dance partner. The announcer continued to do this until all such gifts had been distributed. When the next Round or Gift Dance Song was sung, the ones who were chosen as partners in the last dance returned the compliment to their former partners by taking them up to dance and giving them presents in return. These gifts would be of about equal value to the first gifts. They didn't have to be better. Choosing a partner did not mean they were married; nor did it mean that they would stay together afterward, it was simply for the pleasure of the dance. Women gave things like beaded bags, belts, blankets, and shawls; men gave money, a cow and a calf, a horse, or a blanket. They didn't care what they gave. If the people had nothing else to give, they gave clothing. As the years went by, the giveaways got out of hand. The people started trying to out do one another on the gifts, and this caused family arguments. Then the Head Chief outlawed this practice. This dance of the gift was called čn̓x̣nwe [taking someone by the arm] and the name of the Round Dancing was called snšlšlčmncu.

34

At the end of most War Dances, a dance was done as a Prayer Song for the meal, blessing the food of wild game. There were two versions of the dance. The first could be very long depending on the number of dancers participating, generally from four to eight dancers. The second was shorter and consisted of one to three dancers. This dance was called snčučawmn [Prayer Song]. In recent years, the people called it the Coffee Dance. Because of the popularity of coffee among the Indians, coffee took the place of broth from wild game.

As the first and longer of the Prayer Songs began, there were four dancers, two on one side and two on the other. In the middle of the four dancers was a pot of meat, broth, or coffee. They would extend their arms forward and skyward while War Dancing in one position. One dancer would carry a stick, one to two feet in length. When the song began the fourth start, they danced towards the middle with their arms still extended. The two dancers from one side touched the hands of the dancers from the opposite side above the pot. Then they danced backwards to their original places. The dancer who carried the stick danced sunwise

35

around the pot in the middle and returned to his original position while the other dancers remained dancing in their places. The eighth start of the song was danced the same as the fourth start. When the dancer with the stick danced around the pot in the middle, he was joined by one of the dancers from the opposite side, and then they returned to their original places. On the twelfth start, the dance was the same as the fourth and eighth starts. When the dancer with the stick danced around the middle again, he was joined by his teammate plus the dancer from the opposite side. This left one dancer remaining dancing in position. The group returned to their positions. The sixteenth start they danced to the center, met, and danced backwards to their original positions. Then all four danced around the pot in the middle. The one with the stick broke away from the other dancers and danced next to the pot in the middle. At any time the dancer with the stick wished, he could end the dance by poking or hitting the meat, or poking the stick into the broth or coffee. Then the dance was over. The drum was hit loud and sharp with one beat followed by a rolling beat which gradually faded out.

The second Prayer Song or Coffee Dance was a shorter version of the first, except for a different song and fewer dancers. As the song began there were, for example, three dancers with the pot of broth or coffee in the middle of the dance arena. Two dancers were positioned side by side in the middle about ten feet away from the pot. A lone dancer carrying a stick was at the opposite side of the pot, the same distance away. Before the song began, there were four solid beats on the drum. Then the drumming began at a fast rolling beat. At this time, the two dancers danced stationary, with their arms extended forward and skyward. Their hands were open with palms facing towards the pot in the middle. The single dancer danced left to right, back and forth in a small area, and made the sounds of a prairie chicken, "Hip, hip, hip, hip." When the drum beat changed from the fast rolling rhythm to a single beat as a War Dance Song, the dancers danced towards the middle and then crossed over exchanging places. The song started over again. The dancers danced the same as the first time to the fast rolling beat and exchanged places again. This was done through four starts of the song. Then the dancer with the stick poked the stick into the pot of broth or coffee at the end of the fourth start or verse and the dance ended. There was a solid beat of the drum, followed by a rolling beat which faded out shortly.

The final song of the celebration was called snpx̌ʷnmcu [the Separation Song, better known as the "Home Sweet Home Song"]. As we began our celebration with prayer, we closed with the prayer song of Home Sweet Home. The prayer was that everything that had been performed would be protected, that all the people would be blessed with happiness, good health, and good fortune, and that everyone would be around for next year's gathering to bring back the memories of our ancestors.

Showing Good Respect
Changes in the Arlee Powwow
interview with Johnny Arlee

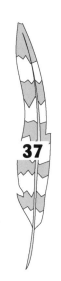

The powwow is not an entertainment or a time to make money. It is a celebration: calling the people to come and share, and thanking the people for coming. Many of us on the quiet side pray before the powwow starts. We have our sweats and pray for a successful powwow. The prayers are that everyone works together in harmony, so that, at the end of the powwow, everybody can say they had a good time and want to come back next year.

When the people come onto the grounds, they can know that the powwow has already been prayed for. We have prayed to Grandfather that everyone who comes to dance, gamble, visit, or just watch and relax will lose their heaviness and be involved in the good feeling of the powwow. As Pete Beaverhead told us, it is the people who make the powwow. Some might gamble, others dance, and others watch, but all the people there make the powwow. The powwow is a once a year ceremonial; a calling people together, a time that the Indian people give; it is a gift.

It should not be a question of the money. Even the contesting should be seen as a give away. And what you give away always seems to come back to you. If our people win the contest, that is good; but the visitors help make the powwow.

The children who dance need to learn that the outfits they are wearing are not just clothes. They should know what they are imitating in their dancing and what their outfits represent. When a person makes an outfit or it is put away, they are just material things. But when it comes time to dance, the people who dance bring the outfit alive. It is like a priest who has a prayer for each part of his vestments and kisses it to show his respect. I see many little kids getting good training to put their stuff away when they are not wearing them and not leave things around. They are learning to show good respect. I do not believe little kids should have eagle feathers in their outfits because they can play around in them and abuse them and not show respect.

**Johnny Arlee
about 1950**

My Early Years

I was raised with Eneas Granjo. He used to have a dance troop during the 1950s, and we went to pageants in Three Forks, Bozeman, Missoula, and Stevensville. We did a lot of traveling off the reservation. The dance group included the Ninepipes, the Big Sams, Harry and Cecile Felix, John Adams, and others. Granjo used to bring out some of the old dances to reenact, such as the Coffee Dance, the Scalp Dance, and the Scout Dance.

He also used to run the Arlee Powwow, sometimes with Vic Matt, Vic Lumpry, or others. I remember Potsey Lumpry riding his horse into the dance pavilion as the scout. He had a blanket tied around his shoulders and, with the wind blowing, he looked like Superman to me. They sang the song to greet the scout as in the early powwows.

In the 1950s, nearly all the dancers had war bonnets, beaded vests, pheasant feather round bustles, and arm bands. You very seldom saw a porcupine roach. The few dancers with roaches were usually from Browning. Even as a young boy of about ten years old, I was wearing a war bonnet that Granjo had made for me.

Granjo asked Joe Big Sam to make my war bonnet. Joe had me come up and sit with him while he made it. I never did anything but sit and watch him put the war bonnet together. Later I was able to make a war bonnet by remembering how Joe had constructed mine. It was a spotted eagle war bonnet.

Granjo had a friend from Browning who came to our camp. He asked to trade his roach for my bonnet. He asked Granjo, but Granjo said it belonged to Johnny so he would have to deal with me. I liked the roach because it was something different. I looked at Granjo, and you could almost tell on his face, "Don't do it." But I wanted the roach, so I made a deal for it. Later I found out that I got the raw end of the deal because the eagle feather bonnet was much more valuable than the roach.

Today you very seldom see a war bonnet, and almost everybody has a roach. Also in the 1950s, most of the dancers had pheasant feather round bustles and leg and arm bands. Not many had eagle feather bustles.

In the 1950s, Granjo got rations for the campers at the powwow. He went to Missoula to Eddy's Bakery and got the day-old bread. He knew some of the farmers in the Bitterroot Valley and got potatoes from them. He had certain people before the powwow who would hunt wild game for the rations. He would reimburse them for their gas and expenses out of his own pocket. This way there was always enough food for the celebration.

You never saw kids running around in the middle of a war dance or a stick game in those days. Especially not in a stick game. A stick game is a time of battle, two teams fighting each other. The stick game was the only time you were allowed to point at somebody. A kid could get hurt by all the pointing and competition between the sides.

People then were careful not to be rude. When you passed by someone in the back, you always said, "I'm coming behind you." If you crossed in front of someone you made a sign. You made people aware so they knew what your intentions were.

When I was young, I could not leave the dance floor until the end of the dance, about midnight. The Canvas Dancing started even before the end of the War Dance. After the War Dance was over, I got permission to go out Canvas Dancing and grabbed a blanket and ran out to the camp. The encampment was in a circle—everything was in a circle. Then we danced and sang until someone came to get me shortly before daylight. I went back to camp to sleep and would not even remember them coming around singing the Wake-up Song.

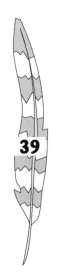

39

Traditions

A long time ago it was different from the times I remember as a young man. Each item of the outfit was made from instructions from the spirits. They really had pride in what they wore. Many parts of the dance regalia were remembrances of battles or personal acts of bravery.

The young dancers today need to learn about their background and their ancestors—the ones who made it possible for them to be dancing today. I do not know what our ancestors would do if they saw what we are doing today. The children should be taught what their values are, the purpose and meaning of their outfits. Then they will be able to talk about these things and teach their children not to abuse things.

Today lots of kids get hurt if they do not win. They cry and stomp around the floor. They need to be taught the real meaning of their dancing and the celebration.

40

Recent Powwows

In the 1960s we started having an MC or Master of Ceremonies. Today we are spoiled. We wait on the MC to tell the dancers when to get dressed and the drummers when to get ready. One time I was sitting with Aaron Perry at St. Ignatius waiting for the powwow to start. Several powwows were going at the same time, and it was getting on seven o'clock and no one was there.

Aaron asked me, "What are we going to do?"

I said, "I don't know."

"Should we get dressed?"

"I don't know," I replied.

After a while we started chuckling. We had become spoiled. We needed an MC to tell us what to do. Today the MC runs the whole floor.

I remember when the War Dance Chief danced in the opposite direction around the outside of the dance arena. He checked to see if dancers were sitting down. If he saw you sitting down, he would hoop or holler at you as he danced past. If he came back around again and you were still sitting there, he had a whip in his hand and he would snap you with it.

Today, it is like being at a rodeo. We have a grand entry and a grand exit. The announcer tells you everything that is coming up.

In the early 1970s, we started forming the powwow committees to clean up the powwow grounds. The powwow had become known as a beer garden place. The committee worked to dry it out and put police at the gates to check for alcohol and keep it out. We got flack over that.

It took three years to clean up the powwow from alcohol. It has cut down on the arguments, fighting, and disrespect. Today, the powwow is pretty clean. It is honorable again to be Indian.

We wanted to do away with paying the dancers in the 1970s, but the elders on the committee objected. In the 1950s, Granjo would collect $.75 a head from the non-Indian visitors at the gate and pay the dancers $2 or $5 each. This was not originally really pay for dancing, but a thank you. The people got the idea they had to be paid. The money really spoiled the people.

The encampment in the 1950s was in a circle. Everything was in a circle. I can just about remember where everyone had their camps. Now everybody is camped all over the place. We tried in the 1970s to get some kind of order and put the camp back in a circle. We were bumping heads with everybody. People insisted on being able to camp wherever they wanted. You cannot tell anybody anything now. There is no respect anymore.

They no longer give out rations to campers at Arlee. Nobody cooks anymore, and some of the committee members got upset because they saw the meat and other food spoiling in the garbage. My wife, Joan, really liked the rations in the late 1970s when she first came to Arlee. They were something good, something you could eat. Now they only hand out trash bags at Arlee, but some other tribes still give out rations at their powwows.

Johnny and Joan Arlee

41

Now you see some professional dancers doing the circuit from powwow to powwow. Their hearts are not really in it. Anything to do with the money is not traditional. I get so upset sometimes today. Everything is oh so sacred. There are so many special restrictions, but it is a whole different idea with money involved in it.

Dancers come in from different places who are only in it for the money. They do not dance every dance. During the contest dances, they put on their best show for the judges and that is all. They hit and run.

One time down in Pullman, Washington, I was with my dad's drum. We saw this dancer from Browning who lost a feather right by us. He just picked it up, put it in his mouth, and kept on dancing. Then he went on and won the entire contest. The value of traditional things does not mean anything to dancers like that. Most dancers are honest. If they drop anything during a contest, they pick it up and walk off the floor. Others are just there for the money. It is sad.

In my generation, we had shows and exhibitions at the powwow. Now we come into the age of the contesting. I wonder what is going to happen in the future and worry about the kids today who grow up and do not learn the purpose of different traditions at the powwow. What are they going to be able to pass on to their kids?

Salish Indian Celebration Dances

by Johnny Arlee

Owl dancers showing men's and women's traditional outfits.

Traditional Salish Celebration Dances in the Order They Are Performed

Memorial Dance: Many years ago, there were many songs that were sung for the Memorial Dance. On the first day of the celebration, children were told not to be noisy or shout while they played. This was the day to honor the loved ones who had passed away. During this time, persons who had special inheritances would join in a procession which was led by one of the spiritual leaders. The people would be wearing or carrying items which were Memorial Keepsakes. The encampment would shed tears in memory of their loved ones. After the procession was finished, the announcement was made, "Leave your sorrows, it is now time to celebrate for happiness."

Snake Dance: The Snake Dance was done to begin a War Dance. It was led by a chosen man who gathered the dancers at a designated spot, generally at the camp of the Chief of the celebration. The dancers danced in single file towards the war dance pavilion with the leader weaving and doubling back in the fashion of a snake. The drummers and singers followed the group singing the Snake Dance Song.

Grand Entry: A special song was sung by the tribe in order to begin the War Dancing. In later years, this dance has worked well for the Master of Ceremonies to introduce dancers and guests from different tribes.

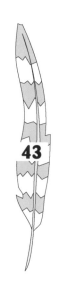

43

Flag Song: The Flag Song is treated with respect; it is as important as the national anthem is for the non-Indian. The Indian flags were made of eagle feathers attached to a long staff or spear and were carried by great warriors. The Indian flag was equivalent to a diploma, certificate, or trophy. The song was sung to open each performance.

Intertribal Dance: Everyone is welcome to dance in an Intertribal Dance. You don't have to have a dance outfit and you can dance in street clothes. Please join the dancers.

War Dance: Each warrior had his own style of dancing. A great number of songs are sung for War Dancing. There are fast and slow War Dances. The elders of the tribe say the older style of War Dancing was similar to the Crow Hop.

Women's Traditional Dance: The Women's Traditional Dance consists of remaining stationary and bending the knees with a slight up and down movement of the body. Most traditional dancers wear or carry a shawl, and some carry an eagle or hawk feather fan or a single feather.

Men's Traditional Dance: The Men's Traditional Dance is held over from times when war parties would return to the village and "dance out" the story of a battle, or hunters would return and dance their story of tracking an enemy or prey. The outfit of the traditional dancer is more subdued in color than some of the other dancers. The outfits are frequently decorated with bead and quill work, and traditional dancers wear a circular bustle of eagle feathers, representing the cycles and the unity of everything.

Man Fancy Dancer

Round Dance: The Round Dance, which is also called the Circle Dance, is a happy social dance because it is meant to get everyone to participate. The Gift Dance was also done during the Round Dance. When one person wished to give a gift to another, he merely escorted the person inside the circle of dancers and began Round Dancing around the drum. When the song ended, the gift was presented. Generally, an announcement was made as to what was given, who received it, and who gave it.

Scout Song: When a scout returned to the camp with news, he would ride back and forth outside of camp making the howling song of a dog or a wolf. The encampment, upon hearing this, would gather at the edge of camp and begin to sing the Scout's Song. When the scout approached, he would be hit lightly with a stick by the leader. The scout would then signify by a signal whether he had seen something human or animal. He would be asked for his news, and then he would tell what he had seen.

Scalp Dance: The Scalp Dancing was done by the women who were dressed in men's clothing. After battles, the men would return to camp with scalps which were tied to the end of the stick. There was a specific song that was sung for a group of women to go to certain camps to prepare for the Scalp Dance. Another song was sung when the women were being painted up and entering the war dance pavilion. There are many songs that are sung for the Scalp Dance. Gradually some of the women would leave the group. When they returned, they would be dressed in old, ragged clothing; their faces were darkened with ashes, and each carried a stick. If one of the women placed her stick over the shoulder of a man, and it was not pushed away, the two were considered married.

Lost Article: A song was sung to gather the warriors who were to tell of their great deeds. In the Lost Article Dance, items were left on the ground; the dance ended when the warrior picked up the last item. The warrior then told of how he had taken certain items during the battle. There were

Woman Fancy Dancer

45

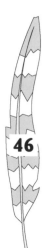

many warriors who had stories to tell of their great deeds. When the stories were finished, a certain song was sung to signify that the Lost Article Dance had ended and for the warriors to be escorted out of the dance circle.

Prairie Chicken Dance: Many years ago a man resting in a field woke and heard singing near him. Very carefully he raised up and saw the prairie chicken singing and dancing in prayer. The man returned to his people and showed them how this dance was done. The dancers strut around and show off as the prairie chicken. In later years, this dance became a speciality and it is used much in competitions because it has a different style of drum beat.

Canvas Dancing: When a warrior prepared to leave on a hunt or raiding party, he would begin by singing at one camp and then go on to the next, singing a different song at each camp. Others would join to help the warrior. The group grew larger and, before the first light of morning, the group would be gone without a word said. So, if one walked around the encampment in the late hours of the night, you might hear a group of people singing Canvas Dance songs from camp to camp.

Home Sweet Home: This farewell song is the closing prayer song which was sung at the end of the celebration. As the celebration began with a prayer, we close it with a prayer. Today, the Home Sweet Home Song is sung after each day's performance.

Jingle Dress Dancers

46

Grass Dancer

Some Newer Dances at Salish Celebrations

Fancy Dance: This very colorful and exciting dance is used in championship dancing. It allows many of the younger dancers to demonstrate their various steps and fancy movements. The dance judges have their work set out for them; they judge the dancers on their style and how well the dancers know the song. The dance is based on the "double step" but features fancy footwork, speed, and acrobatic steps and motions.

Jingle Dance: According to one story, the Jingle Dance evolved from Mille Lacs, Minnesota. Four women wearing jingle dresses appeared to a holy man in a dream. Upon awakening, he and his wife made four dresses and told people about the dream and the dance. The jingle dress is not likely to be mistaken for anything else. The dress is made from cloth with 365 metal cones or jingles covering it.

Grass Dance: This dance came from the Blackfeet and other Plains tribes. One story of the origin of the dance tells of a vision received by a crippled man who could not dance the War Dance but was able to perform the swaying step that moves the many fringes on the Grass Dance outfits.

Owl Dance: This social dance was introduced in the early 1900s. The drummers and singers move to the center of the arena. Couples dance together with men on the outside and move around the drum in a circle.

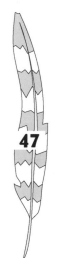

47

Drumming and Singing Group

Images and Memories
Arlee Fourth of July Celebration about 1940
photographs by Rex C. Haight

Snake
Dance

Opposite page and above: Three views show Snake Dancers opening a War Dance session. They dance single file from the camp circle into the arena. **Right:** The Nine-pipe Drum and singing group accompany the Snake Dance. Individuals are identified on page 61.

First page of photo essay: Two views of the Fourth of July camp circle.

Stick Games

Views of a stick game, a common Indian gambling game. **Opposite page:** Kneeling players form two opposing teams. The team on the right-hand side is singing their stick game song and beating on the long pole on the ground while hiding the bones. **Above:** The player with the clenched fists is hiding the bones. The opposing team must guess which hand has the unmarked bone. The sticks won so far in this game are stuck upright in the ground. **Left:** View of another team of stick game players singing and hiding the bones. **Right:** Eneas Granjo, a leading figure in Arlee Celebrations. Identifications, page 62.

Spectators of various ages enjoying the war dances. Identifications, page 62.

Spectators

Cooking, drying meat, and household duties at camp.

Camp Scenes

Young at heart

Above left: Chief Martin Charlo and family. **Above right:** Mr. and Mrs. Pierre Adams. **Lower left:** Baptiste "Potsey" Lumpry in suit and in traditional dance outfit. See page 62 for more information.

Children are the center of Salish celebrations. **Left:** Paul Felix, Sr., wears a porcupine roach headdress. **Below:** Pat Adams wears an eagle feather headdress. **Right:** Two views of mother and child in cradleboard.

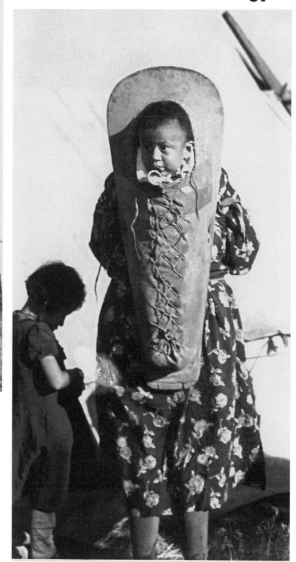

Children

The celebration is an exciting time of learning and friendship for the children. From discovering images on paper (above left and lower left) to horseback riding and meeting a canine friend, the celebration has special memories. Top right: Far right figure, Francis McDonald (the other boys are unidentified).

Hot July days call for
cool aquatic adventures.

Photographs by
Rex C. Haight

The photographer for this trip to the 1940 Arlee Fourth of July Celebration or Powwow was Rex Cassidy Haight of Missoula. He was born in Iowa in 1892, the sixth son in a family of ten boys. He served in the U.S. Navy in World War I and graduated from the Iowa State Teacher's College in Cedar Falls, Iowa. In 1919 he married Sylvia Ufford in Cedar Falls and the couple moved to Montana. Haight worked as an administrator and athletic coach at a series of small Montana schools: Victor, Forest Grove, Denton, and Grassrange.

He then moved to Helena where he organized the new state correspondence school for isolated rural Montana students. The school also supplied specialized correspondence courses for small rural high schools that did not have enough students to be able to hire teachers in all subject areas. In the late 1930s he moved to Missoula and operated the correspondence school in affiliation with the state university.

In 1937 or 1938 he suffered a serious heart attack and turned to photography as a hobby. He was especially interested in photographing Native American life and customs. A second heart attack in 1943 killed him. He was survived by his wife and two sons.

The photographs reproduced here were selected from the collection of the Montana Historical Society Photograph Archives in Helena, Montana. They are reproduced here with the generous permission of the Montana Historical Society. For more information about Rex C. Haight see the Haight collection at MHS [photo numbers 954-671 to 954-749] and his obituary in *The Daily Missoulian,* December 23, 1943, page 3, column 1.

Picture Identifications

Not all the individuals outlined or numbered have been identified.

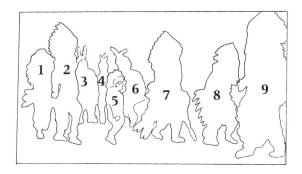

Page 50. Bottom: 1. Pat Adams, 3. Pete Beaverhead, 5. Paul Felix, Sr., 7. Pierre Andrew, 8. Louie Combs, 9. Sam Finley.

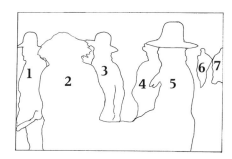

Page 51. Bottom: 1. Louie Ninepipe, 2. Eneas Granjo, 3. Tony Quequesah, 4. Frank Antoine, 5. Happy Ninepipe, 6. Louise Vanderburg, 7. Cecile Hewankorn.

62

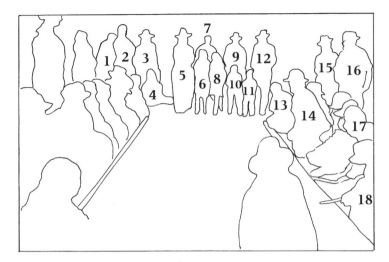

Page 52. 5. Louie Paul, 13. Agnes Curley, 14. Philip Kallowat.

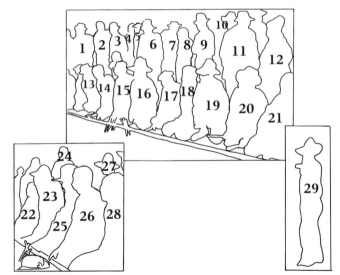

Page 53. Top: (Standing) 2. Joe Antiste, 4. Lawrence Finley, 5. Frank Antoine. (Kneeling) 9. Louie Gingras. 10. Pete Pierre. 12. Mary Susan Finley. 13. Tom Lozeau, 14. Mary Charlo. 15. Tony Charlo, 16. Philip Kalowat, 17. Ed Lozeau, 18. Johnny

Finley. Lower left: 22. Louie Quintah, 24. Katie Gebeau, 25. Eneas Conko,   26. Louie Hammer. Lower right: 29. Eneas Granjo.

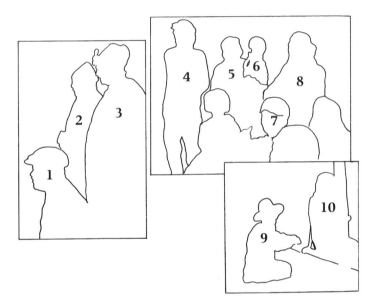

Page 54. Left: 2. Madeline Delaware, 3. Josephine Couture. Upper right: 4. John Lumpry, 5. Annie Stanislaw, 8. Penama Pierre. Lower right: 9. Pasho (last name not known).

Page 56. Top left: Chief Martin Charlo and family. Back row, left to right: Mary Charlo, Mike Charlo, Martin Charlo, and Tony Charlo. Front row: Vic Charlo and Gene Charlo. Martin Charlo was the traditional chief of the Salish Flathead Indians. Top right: Mr. and Mrs. Pierre Adams. Mrs. Adeline Adams was the daughter of Jackson Sundown, the famous rodeo rider.

Other Voices

Salish Celebrations as Seen from Other Parts of the Circle

63

It Was Good: The Indians Did a Lot of Work
interview with Pete Beaverhead

When the smallpox epidemic hit the Indians, we contracted it here [St. Ignatius] first, then the Salish [at Arlee]. The Flatheads [at St. Ignatius] were told not to go visit. That's why they had the July celebration over here. The next year they held the celebration over by Moiese. The pow-wow.... We don't say powwow, we just say čulay.

Now, when they were first planning the July celebration, Chief Qeyqeyši called a meeting in June to discuss the upcoming celebration. Everyone gathered, including the ones who owned a lot of cattle, like the McDonalds. They were told they could donate a beef for the celebration. Each person got up and talked until everyone had a say in the planning. Remember the price of food was cheap back then. Five pounds of sugar was 75 cents, 50 pounds of flour was 90 cents. Today it is high. All the Indian people put down money, so they had a lot—several hundred dollars—and that was used to buy coffee, sugar, salt, and baking powder for the celebration. The ones who owned lots of cattle each said, "I'll give a big cow." So then they had lots of meat. Now, during the celebration, the person designated to buy the food would do so early in the morning. About three of them would go in a wagon. They kept the donated cattle at Joscum's corral. They killed the cows there, then brought the meat over and started distributing it to the camps. It was good. There was lots to do during the čulay celebration. The Indians did a lot of work. Nowadays all they do is play stick game and cards. Those days it was different; there were no stick games. [Feb. 25, 1975]

Sam Resurrection Brings the War Dance

Then we finally got the War Dance, which came about not too long ago. Sam Resurrection went to Cheyenne, or some place, and watched War Dancing. When he got back to Arlee, he taught the Indians how to

Pete Beaverhead (1891–1975) was a well respected elder of the Salish tribe. He left many tapes at the Salish Culture Committee describing traditional Salish ways.

War Dance. He went over to the Ronan area, and the Indians liked the War Dance there, too. All he had was some bells to dance with. He'd say, "This is how it's done," and pretty soon somebody would get up to dance and sing along. He had three War Dance Songs that he sang. They'd dance three days in Ronan. It got so the dancers would take apart clocks for the shiny parts and cut them up for decorations. To look around today and see the costumes that are made for War Dancing. Boy, they're sure nice, the fancy beadwork and all. [Mar. 14, 1975]

We Ran Out of Pocket Watches

Sam Resurrection put on a dance, and the Indians celebrated. He told the people, "We will cook and eat at midnight." The women cooked bitterroot, moss [sqʷĺa], and baked camas. They also had deer meat that was pounded.

Sam Resurrection taught the War Dances until we learned how to do it right.

The young boys and men began to make costumes. In the beginning, they didn't wear pants very often. When they danced, they all wore leggings. Even when they only had a few bells on, it was considered good enough to join in the War Dance.

The Indians took their pocket watches and took the round shiny back part off the watches. They cut it a certain way and smoothed it out and put it on their costumes. They also used yellow brass. They cut and filed them and tied them on and used them as arm bands.

We would all look at the costumes and think they were nice. Finally, one day we saw one person wearing a small hair roach [sncĺa]. We really envied him. Then the Indians started to make headdresses [ćlqey]. They took twelve beads and strung them and tied them on with something red. It was good. We Indians from Crow Creek ran out of pocket watches. [Feb. 28, 1975]

Sam Resurrection (1857–1941) was a cultural and political leader of the Flathead Reservation Salish during the early twentieth century.

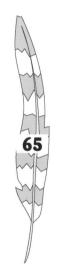

65

The Man Who Raced His Shadow

At the racetrack, people knew who the fastest ones were for the fifty-yard and one-hundred-yard dash. There was one man at Camas Prairie who thought, "I'll do some running so I can surprise them during July at the races."

So when the sun went down, he'd run. He ran quite a little ways, and real early in the morning, he ran again. He ran well.

He thought, "Yoh, I'm fast." When he got back from running, he wouldn't be stiff or sore.

As it got nearer to July, he thought, "Now I'm ready, I'm fast. I'm going to try running during the day."

That evening he went to try it. He had his shirt off and thought, "I'll just go one way in a straight line to a goal."

He ran. As he was running, his shadow came alongside of him. That's what he was watching. The harder he ran, the more it seemed his shadow was getting ahead of him.

66

The next evening, again it was the same.

The next day he thought, "I'm going to try not to eat this evening. Maybe it's from my eating that my shadow beats me."

So he did not eat that evening. The time came; he raced his shadow. At the finish he just barely beat his shadow. His shadow was a little behind him. As he was nearing the finish line, he turned a few degrees away from his shadow. That's why he thought he beat his shadow.

He thought, "Now no one can beat me."

Soon it was July.

He walked around the camps saying, "Hoh, anyone who thinks they are fast in the one-hundred-yard dash—and I'm talking to all of you, to my people, to the Kootenais and any other tribe—here is my money, here is my blanket, here is my saddle. I'm going to bet it all."

So the people made their bets. The race was starting.

He was already happy. He thought, "Hi yoh, I will win a lot of things. I'll make fools of them. No one knows I've been practicing running."

They asked him how he wanted the race to start. "Did you want to start with a gun shot or have someone yell 'Go'?"

He said it did not make any difference to him. "Ask my opponent which he prefers."

His opponent said, "Just yell 'Go.' That's good enough. Tell us 'Go' and we'll run. There will be a winner. Even if you don't start at the word 'Go,' I'm going. You will be the slow one."

The race began. From the very beginning, his shadow was ahead. While watching his shadow, he [the guy from Camas Prairie] tried to run hard, but he tripped and fell. He jumped up and ran to the finish line, but could not win. He lost [to both his shadow and his opponent]; he went broke; lost everything.

This is what one man did. [Mar. 7, 1975]

They Done Me In
interview with Blind Mose Chouteh

A long time ago, during this time [just before Ash Wednesday] we didn't sleep at night. We'd just sleep a little during the day. We'd be War Dancing because Ash Wednesday was nearing.

The longest we danced was eighteen days, every day. I'd drum till morning. The day before Ash Wednesday, we were War Dancing at Lome's. They said we would dance until evening. We danced until daylight, then danced until noon and had lunch. That was the eighteenth and a half day that I had to drum. After I finished eating, I went outside to the toilet. Then I sat on the porch of the kitchen, rolled a smoke, and had a cigarette. As I was smoking, I tried to holler, nothing. I couldn't make a sound. Mali Ketli [Mary Catherine] opened the door and said, "Okay, we're ready to begin. We've already swept the floor." I made a motion to get her attention, to call her over. She came over and stood beside me.

She said, "What?"

I told her, "I can't sing. I can't holler. I can't get myself to be very loud. They done me in."

She said, "Is that true?"

I said, "Yes."

"Maybe your throat will get better later," she told me.

I said, "No." It seemed that my throat was swollen large. I told her, "There are plenty of other singers. They can sing."

She said, "They're not very good. They don't know how to lead songs."

So she went in. Later, Mali Nqaqaa [Mary Canvas Dancing] came out. I told her too. Sam Muti [Sam Moody] came out. I told him also. Antli came out. I also told him.

Antli told me, "Those other drummers are lazy and not very good. I guess that will be all. We might as well break up."

Blind Mose Chouteh (1891–1987) was head drummer for Flathead Reservation powwows for thirty-six years beginning about 1910. He turned blind as a young man but loved to tell stories of the old days. Many of his stories were recorded by the Salish Culture Committee. He was a lifelong resident of St. Ignatius, Montana.

So I was listening when he went back in and made the announcement, "Give me your attention. We will now break up the War Dancing. We finished off our leader. There is no way that his voice will clear up. Even though you other singers are not very good, sit down and sing. We'll dance some more."

No one moved. Their throats were all right, but nobody attempted to sing. So we broke up and that ended the War Dance. [Feb. 15, 1977]

69

They Would Celebrate All Day and Night
interview with Mary Finley

It is right around there—a little further over [by Arlee]—where the July celebrations were held a long time ago by the old Indians. That is where many of the dances were performed or reenacted. The Snake Dance, the Coffee Dance, and then everything else was done. In the [Memorial] Parade the people walked around the camp with the belongings of Indians who had passed away. When that was done, then the čmšmste [scout] would ride around inside of the campground. He would make his horse gallop around until he made one circle around the camp. Then he would go on, singing….They would parade around the camp on foot, singing. It sounded good. Esnunše, they call it; esnunše—memorial. So when it was dark they'd nqaqaa [Canvas Dance]. The Indians, they'd Canvas Dance until it turned daylight because the Indians were enjoying themselves.

Today I heard that sometime, also during the celebration at Arlee, there were some people doing the Canvas Dance, and they were confronted by the police and forced to stop the Canvas Dancing. They were told by the police, "Don't you know that the people are sleeping. You better stop the Canvas Dancing and the singing." This isn't what the police are supposed to be stopping like this. It is the ones that are drunk that he should take care of and stop. They would celebrate all day and night until the next day. The Canvas Dancing would go through the night until daylight. [Sept. 25, 1975]

Mary Finley (1902–1976) was a respected Salish elder at St. Ignatius. She was part of many celebrations on the Flathead Indian Reservation and helped the Salish Culture Committee record stories about tribal traditions.

They All Gather Up and Dance
interview with John Peter Paul

John Peter Paul has been the War Dance Chief for the Salish tribes of the Flathead Indian Reservation since 1982. He has danced at the powwows as long as he can remember. At the Salish Culture Committee, he is working on a history of the Flathead Reservation Salish tribes.

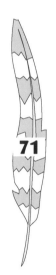

The Fourth of July Celebration is the Indian people's regular big day. They all gather up and dance. Everybody fixes on it each year. Like other doings, they all go for the celebration. It has been important for a long time.

They used to have a Fourth of July Celebration above the [St. Ignatius] Mission. The guy who put on the powwow was called Paul Čulay. [Čulay is the Salish name for the Fourth of July Celebration.] In those days they would dance for ten days with just one drum. There were not many drums in those days. There were no dollars then—no contests like now. The only contests would be when some guy put a nice horse in the dance circle. Instead of raffling it off, they would dance over it. Whoever won the dance competition, got the horse.

We did not have all these dollars. Now you pretty much have to have the contests and dollars, or you would not have anybody come. The way it is now, it is the money. You get a whole bunch of dancers just for the money.

The contests did not begin that long ago. Before that time, we used to have a celebration here [at St. Ignatius] and another one at Arlee. There are pictures of the old celebrations. The tipis were set up in a circle around the encampment. If you had a tent, you had to put it up just outside the circle of tipis.

In those days, the grounds were very clean. Everybody did their share in keeping their own camps clean. The grounds were clean all the time. Now you have to hire somebody to haul the garbage away and even need to hire people to watch the restrooms and keep them clean. The Indians at the celebration used to handle things themselves. They saw that everything was kept clean.

71

Special Powwow Dances

The first day, we have the Memorial Dance to remember those who have died during the past year. We start about seven o'clock and everything is closed, including the gambling joints and stick games. The Master of Ceremonies announces the names of all those who have died so we can look around and remember them. That is important.

One special dance was on the Fourth of July when the old warriors would ride up to the dance area and shoot their guns. Then they dismounted and walked in and began dancing. You do not see that anymore. We still have the Snake Dance on the Fourth of July to begin the dancing. I lead it now [as War Dance Chief]. It takes quite a while.

A long time ago, they had a dance for any feathers or other articles lost on the dance floor. That was when the old warriors would tell about the brave deeds they did during the war. While the warriors were talking, their wives would be piling up blankets and other gifts to give away. We still have the Lost Article Dance. I depend on the veterns to pick up the eagle feathers that are dropped.

72

Other Changes in the Powwow

Now it is a whole lot different from my time. The old people drank, but they had a good time. Now the young people drink and end up in a fight. Young people do not respect anything, so you have to force them to stop. Now everywhere you go, they do not allow alcohol or dope. At all the Indian doings they have police right there to keep that out. It is really nice now that they have eliminated that stuff.

The powwow for me is just having a good time. You count the days when it is coming. The chance to visit one another is the main part of the powwow. People come to the powwow from all over.

The children like the powwow. It was that way all the time, but it has become even stronger. My grandkids are doing good. They enjoy dancing a lot.

What we are doing is teaching the culture. After years pass, you want the kids to take over. Everything we do, we try to get the kids to learn. That is why we have the Salish Culture Committee. I teach the Salish language. On field trips, we try to take as many kids as we can so they can watch and see how things are done.

John Peter Paul

73

You Should Not Forget Your Own Culture, Your Own Tradition
interview with Dolly Linsebigler

The powwow or celebration was always a really important thing for our Salish Indian people. They always looked forward to the big event of July. Many years ago the Salish celebrated by being together, visiting with each other, and dancing.

When the Indian wars were still going on, the Salish had to travel east over the mountains to hunt for buffalo. The buffalo was the food supply that carried them through the winter. They celebrated before they went on the buffalo hunt. I think the reason was because they never knew if they were going to return home after the hunt. That was one of the reasons they celebrated before they left. I think this part is still important today because, just like during the Indian wars, you never know what is going to happen when you leave your home.

I have gone to powwows for as long as I can remember. You go to the celebrations to enjoy yourself and to meet a lot of people—friends and relatives—that you do not ordinarily see. They come to the gathering, and you are happy to see them.

The Importance of Preserving Salish Tradition

Things have changed at the powwow over the years. Being on the Celebration Committee, I feel I should help teach the young people on the committee and those who have not been involved with many celebrations. When they get on the committee, I try to teach them to keep our Salish ways, our own culture, and our own traditions. Although there is some resentment, I still feel that this is what we have to keep doing. The elders who were on the Culture Committee and Celebration Committee back in the 1970s stressed very highly the importance of keeping our own Salish

Dolly Linsebigler has served on the Arlee Powwow Committee since 1976 and has attended the Arlee Powwow since she was a child. She worked at the Salish Culture Committee for seventeen years before she retired in 1992.

74

culture—our own traditions. They stressed that we should not borrow from other tribes things that do not belong here. I have always tried to go along with that. Sometimes, I know that maybe I have been too harsh with it, but I cannot help it. That is the way I am. That is the way I was brought up and what I grew up with. I feel that if we do not do that, our own culture—our own traditions—will not keep going.

For my part, I think the powwow is important. It is especially important for our younger people so they will know our own traditions in the celebrations. It is good for them to learn about all these things. If they are there, they will see all this and observe it. You cannot tell what the kids are thinking. Maybe down the line they will remember what they saw and what they heard and did. Hopefully, somebody will keep it in their mind and tell about it to their own children, their own grandchildren. Then the values we have will keep passing down to the next generation.

Nowadays, people call the powwow just a commercial event. In some ways, I think it is, with everything so modern now. A few people would say that this is the 1990s. And it is true that sometimes we have to move along, but we do not really have to accept the changes. There are a few people who still have the tipis, the tents, and the outfits like the old days. There are a lot of beautiful outfits now. A lot of people call the powwow commercial. The older people would say that there are too many suyapi [white] ways that have been thrown in and that is not right. We are not learning the old ways that our people have taught us.

A lot of things have changed at the celebrations, especially with the contests. I have learned from experience with my own children. When they danced in the contests, it was hard for them, especially when they did not win. I had to explain to them that winning is not important. A couple of my children were threatened when they were in a contest and did win. I always tell my children that the money is not important. The important thing is how you feel about your dancing. You go out there and dance to make you feel better, to drive away your stress and loneliness and bad feelings. When you get out there and dance, you forget about those things. It makes you feel better.

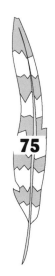

75

The contests change all this. You really have to know the business of dancing now. On the other side, it is good to see the different people dancing and the different categories, but I still do not feel good about the contests. Johnny Arlee has suggested that we have a powwow without contests. I really feel good about that idea. When I saw my dad, my brothers, my uncles, my grandfathers out there dancing, they did not get paid or demand pay. The only pay they got was a soda pop or coffee and that was it. They enjoyed that. They just enjoyed being together and having a good time dancing.

The Work of the Celebration Committee

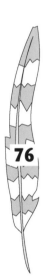

Right now it is so hard to raise money to put on a powwow. It is getting harder and harder. The contests are especially expensive. We have been trying to get different tribal departments to sponsor categories of the contest. A few years ago some did, and it really helped. We go to different businesses to sell ads for the celebration, but some do not buy an ad every year. Some businesses will not buy an ad because they do not go to the powwow.

The Celebration Committee could be a lot better. I would like to see more people involved to take the pressure off those who have been there quite a while. The committee is getting smaller and smaller. We lost a couple of people because they did not have the time to attend the meetings and work at the gatherings. Health is also a part of it for many people. I should have quit a long time ago. I did quit twice! I keep coming back because you do need someone to kind of direct these young people. The committee needs to be reminded to keep our celebrations, our culture, our traditions where they should be.

I talked to the committee a couple of meetings ago. If we really want a good old type of celebration, I would like to see the encampment arranged so all the tipis are in front surrounding the dance arena. All the tents would be put in back the way it used to be. Someone objected that we could not do that. But all we have to do is appoint somebody to take

76

care of that. They could tell the campers that this is how we would like to see the camp arranged at least for one year.

The Importance of the Powwow

As I was growing up, I found a lot of enjoyment because my family were powwow goers. It is one of the things my family has done. We like celebrations. My grandkids are starting to dance now. There are a couple of things that have been put in the celebrations that I do not care for, but I let it slide because these young people enjoy the powwow.

What I would like to see is for our young people, our kids, our Salish people to remember that their dancing is important not only because it is enjoyable, but because it helps them have pride in who they are. You should not forget your own culture, your own tradition. The young people will have to carry this on. It will make the elders that we have left feel better if they know the young people will carry on. The elders will be satisfied with how the young people run the powwow, if the young people stick with their Salish pride and Salish values. I think the old people will be satisfied and feel happy to know that the kids are carrying on.

77

A Lot of People Are Wearing My Craft Work
interview with Oshanee Kenmille

I did my first bead work just before the Fourth of July Celebration when I was eleven years old. It was a little purse with a four-leaf clover on it. I finished beading the four-leaf clover and asked my mom if I could have some beads to fill in the background.

She said, "Let me look and see. If it is good, I will give it to you." So she looked at it and said, "Oh, that is a good job. I'll give you some beads to put in the background." So she gave me some beads. The background was white.

That was my first bead work, seventy-one years ago. Now I am eighty-two years old. I started at that time using the small size 12 beads and I still use size 12. I do not use any other size of beads.

That Fourth of July came, and I was done with the purse. I was showing off to the people at the powwow what I had made.

There was a guy at the celebration that year with a little tiny table with rings, combs, necklaces, and such for sale. He said, "Come here let me look at your purse." He looked at it. "Can I give you some of this stuff for it?" He put down a comb. "Would that be okay?"

I said, "No, no, I can't."

He put down a ring.

I still said, "No, no."

He put down a long necklace.

I finally said okay. And then I went into the dancing area and started Round Dancing wearing that necklace, ring, and comb.

A lot of my bead work and leather work is at the powwow now. When I see that, I feel proud. A lot of people are wearing my gloves. Pat Pierre is wearing a whole outfit I made—vest, leggings, apron, and cuffs.

Oshanee Kenmille is famous for her bead work and hide tanning. She teaches traditional Indian art classes at Salish Kootenai College. Much of her artwork is in use at the Arlee Fourth of July Celebration. She first attended the Arlee Powwow as a young child.

78

Bearhead Swaney has one of the vests I made out of scraps. All the little pieces of leather I sew together.

About fifteen years ago, I started dancing again at the Arlee Celebration. I sit in the same place every year on the north side of the dance arena. So I kept thinking that I better make myself a dance outfit so I would be out there instead of sitting down. I have already changed the skirt twice. It gets dirty, and I have to change it.

The fringes on the arms get dirty and have to be changed often. So I tell people when I make a dress for them, to not have long fringes on the sleeves. I have to change the fringes on my dress before the next Fourth of July.

I drove back and forth clear from Arlee to Elmo [60 miles] everyday during the Fourth of July Powwow. There was one time it was the last day of the powwow, and I did not get any sleep, and it was four o'clock in the morning when everything was done. At the straight stretch of road north of Arlee, I was praying, "Do not let me get sleepy. Let me stay awake. Do not let me drive off the road." I was by myself. I think I was about crying. I saw a falling star come down right where I was going. I came alive; I was wide awake. I started singing all the War Dance Songs. I made it back without being sleepy. I was so happy. I knew that star was helping me.

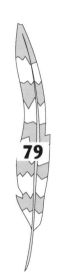

79

I have many projects to finish before the Fourth of July [1998]. I have to make an old-time-style shirt. No cutting, just lace the hides. That goes to Gary Woodcock. He lives in Denver and is going to be here for the Fourth of July Powwow.

There are a couple of guys I am making moccasins for. They are in the army and are going to be back for the powwow. They came to see me during Christmas. I have got to smoke the hides. I have a lot of things to do before the Fourth of July.

The powwow is the only thing the Indians have for their celebration. The white people go to a dance every weekend. The Indians have their celebration only once a year, and they really enjoy it. In the old days, the Arlee celebration was a great big circle of tipis. They put the tents behind the tipis in the circle. They did not scatter the camps all over like they do now. The camps really looked good in a big circle. A long time ago, the Arlee celebration lasted for ten days.

I do not know what to think about the young people today. Many are really interested in dancing. The drugs are really getting some, but I am happy that there are still a lot of the young people interested in the powwow. When you are really into Fancy Dancing, you are out there and you really want to go to it. But when you are as old as I am, you can't. I can't jump high. The dancing really makes me feel like I can jump, but I can't. So the young people should be interested and have a lot of fun dancing. The young people should be out there dancing.

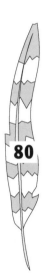

80

We Were Satisfied and We Had a Good Time

interview with Louise Combs

The earliest powwows I can remember were held on the flat just north of Arlee above the Jocko River. We did not have a big dancing pavilion like they do now. We just had a small arena and we had fir boughs for our roof. But we were satisfied and we had a good time. We did not get too hot or wet. At that time, we had only one drum, and the powwow lasted ten days. Some of the drummers would change, and some who did not drum the day before would get in there, but there was only one drum. Now there is a big bunch of drums—big shiny drums. Ours was just a deer hide drum, but we were satisfied with that. The drummers sat on the ground. They did not have stools like they do now.

We had a lot of dancers—young ones and older ones. They had benches for the dancers to sit down on. One guy sitting over on the side had a whip. He was Many Bears, the Whip Man. When they started beating the drum, he jumped up with his whip. Then all the dancers got up ready to go. If they did not want to dance, they just stood there and kept time with the drum until the man with the whip passed them. Then they could sit down again and not get hit with the whip. The dancers kept dancing until they saw the Whip Man sit down. Then the other dancers could sit down if they were tired.

Many years ago they did not dance for prizes like they do now. They did not have any contests. Everybody danced for fun. Now it is all commercial, all for money. It seems like that is what draws the people.

The dance outfits in those days were just buckskin, beads, eagle feathers, and animal hides. Now you see really fancy outfits. I do not like all that fancy stuff. I still prefer the older, simpler outfits.

Louise Combs is 97 years old and the oldest living Salish Indian on the Flathead Indian Reservation. She has attended the Arlee powwow since she was a little girl.

81

When we were celebrating, we kids stayed in our camps and played around there. You did not go into the dancing area in the center unless you went with your parents or grandparents.

A bunch of riders dressed up as clowns would ride up from the Jocko River below the powwow site. They were dressed up in gunny sacks with leaves for their hats. Boy, you should see the kids scatter and run back to their camps. And you stayed in your camp until you saw those clowns go into the dance area. Then you could go back out, but we were too scared. We did not want to go back out any more.

We were really scared of those clowns. Nowadays, I do not think you could scare the kids. I do not like to say so, but people do not watch their kids like they used to. That is why so many accidents happen. The kids get hurt. They get into bad mischief, too. A long time ago we minded. If we didn't, we got the willow stick, and we were scared of that.

They used to have foot races a long time ago at the powwow. They had separate races for the men and women and for fat people and skinny people. They had a lot of fun. Everybody got into the races. They thought it was fun and did not mind being called fat. They would get in there and run. They joined in with pleasure.

They also had a couple of guys called the Dogs. They would ride together bareback on one horse. They sang and shook rattles as they went. They rode around the ring of camps and stopped at each camp. You tied a gift to them or their horse. The gift could be something to eat, something to wear, or something to use.

At first, when they had a store at the powwow, they put it in the ring of tipis. The next year, however, the chief said that was no good. So anyone who wanted to put up a store put it up in the center of the camp circle so it was closer to people camped at different parts of the ring. We had a big ring of tipis. A fellow named Butch Larson had a store at the powwow. He also had a Model T truck he filled up and used to go around to the different camps. He understood a little Indian and could speak a few Salish words.

When you were sound asleep in the morning a bunch of people would come dancing into your camp with their bells, singing a Wake-up Song. You had to wake-up.

Every year when we celebrated here at Arlee, the boys from Fort Hall Reservation in Idaho used to come over. They said they liked to come here because of the river. After they finished dancing, they all ran down to the river and jumped in. That is why they never failed to come. Every time we were going to celebrate here, they came up and had a good time. Others came from the Coeur d'Alene and Nez Perce Reservations in Idaho and from the Kalispel Reservation in Washington.

From other parts of the Flathead Reservation people came in their wagons. They came from Camas Prairie, Elmo, Polson, Ronan, and St. Ignatius. They brought their wagons and camped out here in Arlee.

More Recent Powwows

The last powwows we have had have been pretty good. Not too much of that bottle. They watch at the gate now. That way we have a good time. You do not see broken glass around or drunks.

We try to keep our traditions like the powwow. A lot of young ones do not care much about it. They are not interested, but there are a few who are interested, and we have to encourage them.

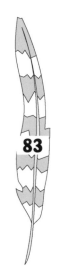

83

The Powwow for Me Is a Very Religious Experience
interview with Bryan Brazill

For me the powwow symbolizes the sacred circle of life. When you dance in that circle, it comes alive. Even the floor becomes alive spiritually speaking. When you dance out there, you dance for the people, for your family. For me the powwow is a very religious experience as it is for a lot of my friends and family members.

Each of the powwow dances has a spiritual beginning and represents the spirits it came from. In understanding that and dancing out there, you respect those beginnings and those tribes where the dances originated. The various dances come from different tribes all over Indian country.

Dwight White Buffalo from the Southern Cheyenne tribe taught me that the Fancy Dance, for example, came from Henry Moore of the Ponca tribe in Oklahoma who had a dream of a stallion. The dance did not come from an attempt to impress non-Indian people or a desire to be very acrobatic. It came from a dream—a spiritual dream. When they dance, the Fancy Dancers represent that stallion.

Grass Dancers dance for those who cannot dance. They represent the crippled and those who cannot get up and dance. The Grass Dance came from a young man from the Omaha tribe who always wanted to dance but was not able to because he was deformed and unable to walk. (This was hundreds of years ago, long before the coming of white people.) The man was told by the spirits to go up to the mountains and fast. The spirits told him that if he followed the dream, he would be able to dance and the Grass Dance would be his. So he did so. When he came back down to his tribe and explained his dream to them, they started singing for him and he started dancing. This is where the original Grass Dance Society started. When this man began dancing, his legs were just starting to move. You

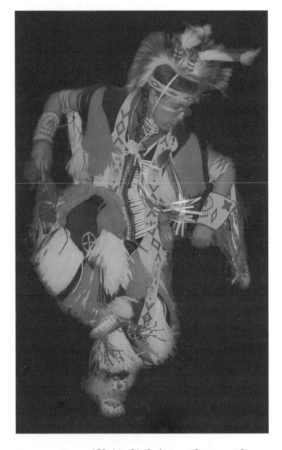

Bryan Brazill (Salish/Northern Cheyenne) from Arlee, Montana, has danced at the Arlee Powwow and other powwows for over thirty years. For about fifteen years he was a fancy dancer, and he has been a grass dancer for the last three or four years. He has taught a class in Native American dancing at Salish Kootenai College. For the last five years he has been a Residential Counselor at Kicking Horse Job Corps Center near Ronan.

can see this in the older style of Grass Dance where the dancer is real low and dragging his legs. Philip Whiteman, Jr., a Northern Cheyenne, shared the story about the origin of the Grass Dance with me.

The Grass Dance spread to other tribes and finally came to the Flathead Reservation about ten or fifteen years ago. It is a dance that is not traditionally part of the Salish tribes, but where it started, it had spiritual beginnings.

All the powwow dances came from spiritual beginnings. The Jingle Dress Dance came from the Ojibwas in Minnesota. A spiritual leader of the Mille Lacs Ojibwas had a medicine dream to make four dresses that made noise. Then he gave these first jingle dresses to four women dancers so they could dance to heal sickness. The Women's Fancy Dance came from the butterfly spirit. Creator gave these dances to certain tribes to take care of, but Creator blessed them so everyone can share them. To me it makes the powwow that much stronger. Some elders frown on the new dances coming in because of the change. But understanding where they came from spiritually, I respect these dances and dancers.

85

Changes in the Arlee Powwow

I remember dancing here at the Arlee Powwow as a young child in the late sixties with just a handful of people and a few drum groups. Then all the dancers were paid one or two dollars for dancing a session. Soon they had contests where first place was paid only about a hundred dollars. A few young men started traveling around the country to different powwows and took turns taking first and second place in the contest. I was really young then—seven or eight years old—and we young guys would really look up to them.

I have mixed feelings about contesting. I made a living at powwows for a couple of years. I did not make enough money to buy a car or a house. In fact, after those seasons were over, I had nothing to show for it except a really good time and having learned a lot. I looked at winning as getting blessed with money so I could keep on traveling and doing what I liked to do.

What made me come full circle and stop contesting was my brother's death. Honoring life, dancing for life, dancing for people who cannot dance, and praying while you dance has become even more important than before. Since then, I have only contested a few times. The one time I did place, I gave all the money away to drum groups and people who needed it.

The Importance of Powwows Today

Powwows are important, but are only one aspect of life. All human beings have basically the same wants and the same needs, such as a place to live, warmth, and food. How we go about getting these things today is pretty much generic in this country for people of all races.

You are able to express your Indianness while you are out there dancing or powwowing or playing hand game. But young people do not learn Indianness from powwows, they learn it from their parents and elders.

At the powwow, the community is not only the community of the location of the powwow, such as Arlee, or even just the Flathead Reservation. The Indian community from all over North America participates in the powwow. You also have family members that are affiliated with the tribe but work far away from the reservation. They come back to the powwow to be around family again.

About 80 or 90 percent of the students I work with at the Kicking Horse Job Corps Center are from southwestern United States tribes. The powwow is pretty new to most of the southwestern tribes, but they have embraced it in a good way. They have brought some of their religious beliefs into how they interpret the powwow. There are powwows all over Indian Country now. The reason it is so popular with the students I work with at Kicking Horse is that it reminds them of home. They really get excited when powwows come around.

You Pray When You Dance
interview with Louie Plant

Louie Plant is an eighteen-year-old fancy dancer from Arlee, Montana. He is a 1998 graduate of Arlee High School.

To me the powwow or celebration is just that—a celebration. It is a whole bunch of people getting together, having fun and enjoying themselves dancing, making new friends, and meeting old friends. From dancing at different powwows, I now have friends all over North America.

Dancing to me is a prayer. You pray when you dance. You pray for those who are ill and sick and pray for those who have passed away. That is what dancing means to me.

I probably started dancing when I first walked. I have been dancing at powwows as far back as I can remember. Even just from the 1980s to today, the powwow has changed a lot. The Fancy Dancing back in the 1980s cannot hold a candle to the Fancy Dancing today. There are more new steps, and the songs are faster now, and the outfits are more elaborate. Back then, things were just plain and simple. Simple is good, and plain is good, but now it is all elaborate, maybe too elaborate.

The meaning of the powwow is different for each person. It depends on what their parents taught them. I do not really worry about the contesting. The contesting and the money have changed a lot of people. I feel most of the dancers are there for the culture and the prayers. They are thankful that they are alive and that they are breathing and that the sun came up that day. A few might be out there just for the money, but many are out there for the culture, and others are out there to enjoy themselves.

I would encourage young children today to get involved and take part in the powwow. The first thing I would tell children starting at the powwow is to have fun. Do not go out to compete, but to have fun and enjoy it—to thank God for life.

87

Pronunciation Guide for
Special Salish Language Sounds

by the Salish Culture Committee

č — like the ch of **ch**ur**ch**.

š — as in English **sh**in.

k̓ʷ — one sound, much as the qu in **qu**it.

c — one sound like the ts of ca**ts**.

q — a k-like sound, pronounced with the root of the tongue raised and retracted.

qʷ — same as q above, but with lips rounded.

ł — voiceless sound produced with the tongue in position for l but without vibrating the vocal cords, and pushing air out around the sides of the tongue.

x̣ — a friction sound produced with the tongue in position to say q above, but with air being forced out, as to clear one's throat.

x̣ʷ — friction sound like x̣ above, but the lips are rounded.

xʷ — friction sound like x̣ʷ above, but the tongue is in position for k̓ʷ.

p̓ — the first of a series of glottalized stops in Salish. Like p, but glottalized. Build up some air pressure below your glottis or voice box, then expel the air forcibly immediately after the release of the p.

t̓ — like t, but glottalized.

c̓ — like c, but glottalized.

č̓ — like č, but glottalized.

k̓ʷ — like k̓ʷ, but glottalized.

q̓ — like q, but glottalized.

q̓ʷ — like qʷ, but glottalized.

λ̓ — one sound, the rapid sequence of t and l, glottalized.

ʔ — the glottal stop can be heard in English between the vowels of "uh-uh" (meaning "no"). It is not distinctive in English, but it is in Salish.

m̓ — the first of a series of glottalized resonants, or prolonged sounds.
　　Pronounced like m, but followed immediately or accompanied by ʔ.

n̓ — like n, but accompanied by ʔ.

l̓ — like l, but accompanied by ʔ.

w̓ — like w, but accompanied by ʔ.

y̓ — like y, but accompanied by ʔ.

90

About the Author

Johnny Arlee is a Salish Indian cultural and spiritual advisor. He lives in Arlee, Montana, on the Flathead Indian Reservation with his wife Joan Arlee from Seabird Island Reserve, British Columbia, Canada.

Born in 1940 at St. Ignatius, Montana, Johnny was raised by his great-grandparents, Eneas and Isabella Granjo in Arlee, Montana. From them he learned to speak the Salish language as his first language and learned about hunting, crafts, and traditional Salish life.

Since September 1996, he has been an instructor for the Salish Kootenai College Salish Cultural Leadership Program. This program allows Salish students to learn Salish traditions by working with elders in an apprenticeship setting.

Eneas and Isabella Granjo

Johnny Arlee

91

About the Artists

Corky Clairmont taught art for nine years in California before returning to the Flathead Indian Reservation in 1984. He is currently head of the Art Department at Salish Kootenai College. His art work, in a variety of mediums, has been exhibited across the United States. He is a member of the Confederated Salish and Kootenai Tribes.

Tony Sandoval, a Navaho artist, was married to a Confederated Salish and Kootenai Tribes member and worked on the Flathead Indian Reservation during the 1970s when he did these drawings for the Salish Culture Committee. He now lives in Cuba, New Mexico, where he works at his art.

Josh Pepion is a member of the Confederated Salish and Kootenai Tribes living in Ronan. A 1997 graduate of Two Eagle River School in Pablo, his artwork has been featured on the covers of two high school yearbooks and one student book of creative writing. The drawing included in this book was part of the prize winning design for the 1998 Arlee Celebration poster. He works mainly in pen and pencil, water colors, and acrylics.

About the Editor

Robert Bigart is Librarian Emeritus at Salish Kootenai College and Director of the Salish Kootenai College Press.